A History of the Bible Lands in the Interbiblical Period

A
HISTORY
OF THE
BIBLE LANDS
IN THE
INTERBIBLICAL PERIOD

ROBERT L. CATE

BROADMAN PRESS
Nashville, Tennessee

ISBN: 0-8054-1154-2
Dewey Decimal Classification: 220.9
Subject Headings: BIBLE - HISTORY OF BIBLICAL EVENTS//BIBLE -
INTERBIBLICAL PERIOD
Library of Congress Catalog Card Number: 88-39528

Printed in the United States of America

Unless otherwise indicated, Scripture quotations are from the Revised Standard Version of the Bible, copyright 1946, 1952, © 1971, 1973.

Scripture quotations marked (NASB) are from the New American Standard Bible. Copyright © The Lockman Foundation, 1960, 1962, 1963, 1968, 1971, 1972, 1973, 1975, 1977. Used by permission.

Library of Congress Cataloging-in-Publication Data

Cate, Robert L.
  A history of the Bible lands in the interbiblical period / Robert L. Cate.
    p. cm.
  Bibliography: p.
  Includes indexes.
  ISBN 0-8054-1154-2
  1. Jews—History—586 B.C.-70 A.D. 2. Jews—History—168 B.C.-135 A.D. 3.
Middle East—History—To 622. 4. Bible—History of contemporary events. I. Title.
DS121.65.C37 1989
933'.03--dc19   88-39528
                                                                          CIP

To Fred
whose concern with the present
has led him to study the past
in order to build a better future

Preface

"Of making many books there is no end, and much study is a weariness of the flesh" (Eccl. 12:12). So the author of Ecclesiastes admonished, and so many a disillusioned student has joined in concluding. That advice is often coupled with a common, cynical attitude summed up by Henry Ford in his 1919 libel suit against *The Chicago Tribune* in which he testified, "History is bunk."

This concept makes many people turn in dismay from any book or study which claims to be concerned with history. That being so, why should I, or anyone, attempt to write another history of anything, much less one dealing with a subject so obviously uninteresting as the interbiblical period, or the time between the Testaments as it is sometimes called? More important, perhaps, is the question as to why you should bother to read this book. Is there anything of value for you here?

These are honest, straightforward questions. They deserve honest, straightforward answers. The reasons for my writing this book are the same ones which should motivate you to read it and to study this era. First, and broadly general, all knowledge is of value. God is the Author of all truth; therefore, any truth is important. Further, if as I believe, this world is the arena of His activity, history becomes the record of His dealings with humanity. If I can perceive how He and people related to one another in the past, I am better able to relate to Him in the present. Hegel, the German philosopher, cynically asserted, and George Bernard Shaw popularized, the philosophy that neither people nor governments learn from history. This simply is not wholly true. We do learn lessons from history. These help us avoid the pitfalls of the present and also warn us of the dangers and unbridged chasms in our future. Only the fool ignores the experiences and lessons of the past. All of this is to say that history is important. It is not bunk.

The second reason for studying this era is more important for Jews and Christians and for anyone else interested in Jewish or Christian origins, history, and development. Depending upon literary and historical conclusions, the Old Testament ended anywhere from about 350 BC to about 165 BC. The New Testament opens about 4 BC and closes in the latter half of the first century AD. In that period between the Testaments, which covers anywhere from one-and-a-half to three-and-a-half centuries, major developments took place. Judaism arose and flourished. Jewish sects and parties developed in Palestine during this era, and Jesus and the early churches had to confront them. Further, the Greek and Roman empires of the period significantly shaped the world of the eastern Mediterranean and affected the development of Judaism and the spread of Christianity. Ignorance of the interbiblical period, therefore, leaves us trying to understand both Judaism and Christianity without an adequate basis. Trying to comprehend either of these by moving directly from the Old Testament is like trying to build a roof over a stone foundation without walls or supports. General shapes and outlines can be seen, but direct connections can be established only with difficulty.

Finally, the period was one of the most exciting times in world history. Forces were at work and developments were taking place which still affect much of Western civilization and culture. Furthermore, as Thomas Hardy suggested, "War makes rattling good history; but Peace is poor reading" (*The Dynasts,* I, vi). If that is the case, this time ought to make good history and good reading, for the interbiblical era had more than its share of armed conflict. Armies marched, battles were fought, kingdoms fell, empires shook, fortresses were betrayed, and national boundaries and influence shifted with the regularity of the ocean's tides. People were born, lived to a ripe old age, and died in time of international turbulence. Many never knew any form of national peace. The times were exciting. Truly, their history does make good reading.

If ever an era cried for peace, this was it. If ever people looked for hope, they did. But tumult was the order of the day for many of the people throughout the era. Hopelessness was their pattern of life.

And life is precisely what this book is about. We are concerned with the great forces of history which transformed a world and shaped a future. But, we are primarily concerned with the results of those movements. Here we search for the difference which the events of history made in the lives of those who lived through those turbulent times. In addition, we will also search for the differences which those days and events have made for us. Join me in the study of these terrible, fascinating, exciting, tumultuous, and world-shaping times.

Contents

1
Introduction

Understanding the material in any book depends to a large extent upon three things. First, the reader needs to know with what presuppositions the author approached his task. If you do not know my presuppositions, you may never really understand what I have said. You will certainly not understand why I drew the conclusions which I did. Second, the reader must know what limits or constraints have been placed upon this particular work. Books with similar titles and subjects frequently differ significantly due to variations in the period of time or geographic regions considered and the intended readership. Third, the reader needs to know the author's basic sources for the study. This includes both primary and secondary sources. Ultimately, anyone wishing to become an expert must consult the primary sources. However, most who wish to become more conversant with the era can accomplish that by a survey of the better secondary sources.

This introductory chapter is intended to identify these factors. I first shall seek to describe the values and purposes of this study as I perceive them. Here I also shall attempt to set forth the presuppositions which guided me. Next, I will identify the temporal and geographic limits which I have set. So that these will not seem utterly arbitrary, I will attempt to explain my choices, recognizing that some scholars will hold other opinions.

Finally, this introductory chapter will list and briefly describe the primary sources. I hope you will at least look up some of these primary sources, whether or not you read them in detail. The better secondary sources are listed in my bibliography. I have kept specific source references to a minimum. Those who are familiar with the field will recognize my indebtedness to many who have gone before; those who read further in the field will make the same discovery. My bibliography is not exhaustive. Rather it is quite selective, being generally limited to those relatively modern works which should be available in most good theological or historical libraries. The reason for this limit is not that I am prejudiced against older works but that the more recent publications incorporate the significant discoveries made since World War II. The Dead Sea Scrolls, for example, have added major new dimensions to our understanding of much of the period. Books written before their discovery simply lack the information which the scrolls supply, thus their data is incomplete and their conclusions may be suspect.

Value, Purpose, and Presuppositions

Value

For most Protestants and Evangelicals, the period between the Old and the New Testaments is marked by little more than a blank page in their Bibles. Even Roman Catholics and the few Protestants who have the Apocrypha tend to read it seldom. In any case, these books do not seriously purport to cover the gap. For the Jew, the Hebrew canon of the Scriptures closes with 1 and 2 Chronicles. (Although they have the same thirty-nine books in their Bible as the Christian Old Testament, they are in a different order.) Most Jews, it is fair to say, know as little as most Christians about the interbiblical period. Yet, for both Jew and Christian, the era is of extreme importance. To understand either Judaism or Christianity fully we need to know what happened in this period and its ultimate and lasting significance and impact.

Purpose

My purpose is to survey the events of the interbiblical period in an attempt to understand how the events shaped the world into which Jesus came. As we understand those molding forces, we can better understand Jesus' life and ministry. We can also better understand the Judaism out of which the early disciples, the apostles, and the Christian community came. We may also better understand why the early Christians were at first a part of Judaism and then were thrust from it.

This book is not an attempt to present a thoroughly detailed history of the period. That is for the scholar. Rather, I am writing for the beginning student. I am hoping that the college student, the busy pastor, and the interested layperson will find guidance and insight. I am also hoping that those who studied this era once, but have ignored it since, will find this to be a stimulating and thought-provoking review. My intent is not to provide new insights or exhaustive inquiries into the minutiae of historical detail. Those who seek this will be disappointed.

Rather, I am attempting to survey the best available insights in the field and to present them in the clearest and most interesting way possible.

No one is more aware than I of my own limitations, or of the limitations of our knowledge of the era. Much is known with certainty. A great deal more is known only as highly probable. Other parts of this history, however, are far less certain; some parts are pure hypothesis. I shall try to stick to the certain and the highly probable. The rest will be treated only lightly. My purpose is not to suggest theories that may have to be changed with the next archaeological discovery. Rather, I seek to build upon certain and solid foundations.

Presuppositions

My presuppositions are simple but very profound because they shape my life, my thought, and my bases for evaluating evidence. First, I am an Evangelical Christian. I believe that Jesus is the Christ, my Lord, the Son of God. Second, I believe that the Bible, both the Old and the New Testaments, is the inspired Word of God. Third, I believe that the other ancient documents from which we get our information about the inter-biblical period, while sometimes written by pious and devoted people, are of a different nature from the biblical materials written in a similar time and by similar people. Fourth, I believe that the historical developments between the Testaments serve as a bridge between them. As we see what happened and what it meant to the people who lived through it, we can better understand the world into which Jesus was born. Further, because of our understanding of what happened between Malachi and Matthew, we can better understand how and why the early churches ministered and served in their world. Fifth, I believe that the informed Christian who wishes better to understand his or her faith needs to know something of the broad sweep of history in this era. In addition, the informed Jew who wishes better to understand the relation between modern Judaism and the ancient Hebrew Scriptures needs to know the developments of the period. Obviously, I have other presuppositions which shape my life. These, it appears to me, are the significant ones which shape this book.

This book is intended for thinking persons who wish to understand their faith better. It covers a link in the chain of religious heritage. It is only a link. Without it, however, there is no chain. With this link we become a part of God's ongoing people, linked to the past and looking to the future.

Geographical Limits

An awareness of geography is as important to the study of history as wind and air currents are to the soaring of an eagle. Historical events occurred in specific places. Hills and valleys, rivers and lakes, deserts, oceans, mountains, highways and cities all affect the course of history. Armies may have been located at two places which appear on a map to have been reasonably close to one another, but an intervening desert or mountain range made them relatively inaccessible to one another. The location of highways frequently determined the routes chosen by conquerors. It is easier to move an army over an already existing highway than to march cross-country, no matter how powerful and well-organized the troops may be, and unwalled cities in a plain fall before an assault far more easily than walled cities located on hills and mountaintops. Further, some pieces of the world's territory are more important to control than others due to their strategic or economic significance. To seek to understand the history of the interbiblical period without a careful study of the physical arena where those events were played out is a task doomed to defeat.

On the other hand, we need to delineate carefully the limits of our geographical study. If we are not careful, we can allow our interest continually to spread in ever-widening circles, like the ripples in a pond. Yet this image suits our study quite well, for our geographical interests in many ways can be viewed as a widening series of essentially concentric circles, just like ripples in a pond. The further we get from the center, the less detailed our concern may be, but each circle must be kept in perspective and in relation to the others.

Jerusalem and Judea

The center of our interest from the beginning almost to the end is Jerusalem, the Holy City of both Jew and Christian. It was here that the second and third Temples were located. This caused the city to be both the religious and the political focus of Judaism as long as Israel endured either as a nation or a province. Of almost equal importance and the over-all center of our concern is that territory known variously as Judah or Judea. Its boundaries varied rather widely throughout the period. At times it was hardly larger than Jerusalem itself. During most of the era, however, it extended northward almost to Samaria, westward to the coastal plain or even to the coast itself, southward almost as far as the Negev or the wilderness, and eastward to the Jordan and the Dead Sea.

Palestine

A larger area of interest includes all of the land bridge which we call Palestine. Bordered on the west by the Mediterranean and on the east by the desert, all land traffic between Rome, Greece, Asia Minor, Syria, and Mesopotamia going to or from Egypt had to move through this relatively constricted region. This made the region economically important, for whoever controlled it controlled a major part of the trade as well as the taxes of the ancient Near East. This region was even more important militarily. While growing amounts of trade were carried by ships on the Mediterranean, significant armies could not yet be so effectively transported. Thus, whoever controlled Palestine to a large extent controlled the movement of troops through that part of the world. No one could control the Near East in the interbiblical period without controlling Palestine. It was just that important.

The Fertile Crescent

Enlarging our concern still further, we must include the Mesopotamian Valley to the northeast and east and the Nile Valley to the southwest. Further, we must also include Syria to the north. This region on a map shows up as a large crescent. Due to the fact that the region is generally fertile due to climate, soil, and rivers, it has come to be designated as the Fertile Crescent. For most of the interbiblical period, Jerusalem and Judah were the scenes of one conflict after another between Egypt to the south and Syria to the north. Each time these armies moved to assault one another, Judah was attacked as well.

Furthermore, at the beginning of the era, the two major powers were Greece or Macedonia to the northeast and Persia to the far northwest. Judah was a Persian province until Persia was defeated by Alexander the Great and his troops from Greece. They swiftly expanded their control of the region to the south and west. Finally, at the end of our period Rome, even further to the west, ruled the world.

The Mediterranean World

These military and empire-building forces of Greece and Rome were surely enough to arouse our concern with their territories. But from the time of the Babylonian captivity (586-539 BC), Jewish refugees began to settle all over the ancient world. While maintaining their racial and religious identity, they also assimilated much of the new cultures where they lived. This group of scattered Jewish settlements permeated the entire world which I have just described. They became known as the Diaspora. Even if nothing else outside of Judah attracted our attention in studying this era, the importance and significance of the Diaspora would do so. They were concerned with what happened in and to their Holy City. Further, as the New Testament era came into flower, the first Christians, and especially Paul, went to the Jews of the Diaspora. Their existence alone draws our attention beyond the boundaries of Judah itself.

Palestinian Topography

Most of our concern is with that region of Palestine centered around Jerusalem and Judea. Let us turn our attention back to that region for a moment.

The region of Judea is essentially divided into four major north-south strips. Along the edge of the Mediterranean is the coastal plain, frequently called the Philistine Plain. Rising sharply to the east is the central highlands. This is a spiny ridge made up of limestone mountains riddled with caves. Further eastward is the great Jordan rift. Here the river Jordan flows from the Sea of Galilee to the Dead Sea, the lowest point on the surface of the earth. Finally, on the other side of the Jordan Valley, the cliffs rise rapidly to the Transjordan plateau, which fades into the Arabian Desert.

Located in the center of the central highlands, Jerusalem was highly defensible. A little to the south and west of Jerusalem lies a wedge-shaped region of foothills between the coastal plain and the central highlands. This is known as the Shephelah. To the far south is the wilderness, known as the Negev. It is barren rocky desert.

The Highways

Through the territory of Judea came three of the four major north-south highways of the Palestinian region. The major highway was the coastal route. It allowed for easy travel of either caravans or armies. The second most important route of the era was generally outside of Hebrew territory proper, moving down the edge of the Transjordan plateau. It was known as the King's Highway. The third highway of importance followed the Jordan Valley, and the fourth came down the central highlands and is known as the water-parting route. The only east-west highway of any significance came across the Jordan from the west at Jericho and made a rapid ascent to Jerusalem. Several other very minor east-west routes came through the region. One of more significance than the others came around the southern end of the Dead Sea and connected all four of the north-south routes.

This, then, is the stage upon which the events of our history were played out. You will find them far more understandable if you remember this broad geographical outline. Even more helpful will be to follow the events on a map. Only by so doing can you more adequately grasp some of the reasons for some of the events we shall study.

Temporal Limits

More important than the geographical limits of any historical study are the temporal limits. As we shall note again and again in this study, history simply does not happen in neatly separated compartments, no matter how precisely we may date major events. Lesser events lead up to and follow as a consequence of major crises. Thus, it becomes difficult to divide one era from another, saying, "This one ends here and that one begins there."

The Beginning

To anyone not familiar with the subject, the interbiblical period appears to be precisely delineated: It begins where the Old Testament era leaves off and ends where the New Testament era begins. However, it is not that simple. Biblical scholars and historians have not reached any consensus as to when the Old Testament era ended. They are not quite as widely separated as to when the New Testament era began. However, great disagreement exists as to whether the interbiblical period overlapped with the New Testament era. Further, if they did overlap with one another, we must then determine the extent of the overlap.

I am quite aware that competent and significant scholars whose judgments have influenced my thinking and whose scholarship I respect will disagree with the temporal limits I place on this study. On the other hand, in order to produce it, I must limit it. I shall at least seek to explain carefully my chosen limits and the reasons behind them.

I conclude that the interbiblical period begins in 333 BC. Two major reasons dictate this from my perspective. First, and by far the more important, is that 333 BC marks the beginning of the campaigns of Alexander the Great in Syria and Palestine. Most historians agree that this marked a major change in the culture and life of the Hebrew people. For this reason, it affords an excellent beginning point for this study. My second reason for adopting 333 BC as the beginning point is related to the first, but is far less significant and clearly more mundane. I wrote an earlier book on the history of the Old Testament era entitled *These Sought a Country: A History of Israel in Old Testament Times* (Broadman, 1985). I drew it to a close with 333 BC. Thus, this book picks up where the other ended.

I am quite aware that some scholars begin their study of the interbiblical era with the rise of Persia (539 BC), while others go back to the time of the Babylonian captivity in the period from 586 to 539 BC. On the other extreme, some consider the period not to have begun until the Maccabean Revolt in 167 BC. Finally, some competent scholars do not believe that there ever was an interbiblical period, considering the Old Testament era to have lasted until the New Testament era began. While admitting the existence of some valid reasons for each of these opinions, I do not believe that they are significant enough to force us to abandon the 333 BC date.

The End

Determining the date for the end of the interbiblical era ought to be more simple and clear-cut, but it is not. Several factors must be carefully considered and evaluated. The New Testament era clearly begins with the birth of Jesus in Bethlehem and with the death of Herod in Jerusalem. These dates are determined by various scholars to be no earlier than 7 BC and no later than 4 BC. If this is when the New Testament era begins, it appears that this should be the date when the interbiblical era ends.

Significant reasons exist, however, for disagreeing with this conclusion. Among these is the fact that not even the birth of Jesus made a great change in what was going on in Jerusalem and Judea. The death of Herod could have done so, but really did not. Even the ministry, crucifixion, and resurrection of Jesus made no obvious, immediate change in the lives of the Jewish people in Jerusalem or Judea, and certainly had no influence on the lives of the Jews of the Diaspora. Thus, while to Christians and to the Bible these events were of paramount and unique importance, their influence began to be felt, even as Jesus described, more like leaven in dough or salt in food. Their influence spread slowly, gently, and only later would people look back and see the ultimate significance of these events. Thus, from a historian's standpoint, they do not offer the kind of break which makes for a good dividing point. From the standpoint of the Hebrew people, life was essentially unchanged over the years marked by the life of Jesus. Even Pentecost and the spread of the gospel by the early churches do not afford any kind of critical break for historians of the era. As important as these events were for world history, they just do not offer a significant dividing line where a major transition took place.

Two events did occur which offer such a critical break: the First Jewish Revolt in the period of AD 66-74, and the Bar Kochba Revolt in AD 132-135. The first led to the Roman invasion of Palestine under Vespasian. Galilee fell in AD 67, Perea and parts of Judea in AD 68, Jerusalem in AD 70, and Masada in AD 74. This was a time of chaos and catastrophe and marked the end of Judea as any kind of independent Jewish state. Some, therefore, consider this to be the end of the era.

On the other hand, most people of the Jewish world still looked to Jerusalem as the religious and political center of their identity. However, with the revolt of Bar Kochba that came to an end. When Rome devastated the region in AD 132-135 as they subdued the rebellion, Judea ceased to exist. Until AD 1948, Jerusalem was the Jews' Holy City only spiritually, and Palestine was their homeland only in history and in hope, not in fact.

Therefore, I have chosen to carry my study of interbiblical history forward to AD 135. I recognize that this entails a major overlap with the study of the history of the New Testament and its era. In treating the period from the birth of Jesus until the end, I shall focus upon the history of the Hebrew people in that time. Of course, where this touched and affected the events of the New Testament and post-New Testament eras, we shall consider it.

Sources

The quality of any history is directly related to the quality of the sources which the historian has available for research and investigation. As I have noted, we possess nothing like an adequate and thorough collection of sources for the study of this era. None of the extrabiblical sources which we possess actually "did" history in the modern sense. At best, the sources which we have are apologies or defenses of particular viewpoints, philosophies, or theologies. At worst, they are propaganda, at times even apparently "creating" or "inventing" history in order to substantiate particular viewpoints or prejudices. The contemporary historian must use these sources critically and carefully, evaluating one against another, and drawing conclusions with care. Obviously, our reconstruction of this historical era can be no better than our sources. Equally as obvious, no reconstruction can be better than the accuracy and adequacy of our critical evaluations and our conclusions. The basic sources upon which any historian of the period bases his or her study are these which I have delineated as falling into ten categories.

Josephus

The most important sources for the knowledge of the era we are studying are the works of Flavius Josephus (ca. AD 37/38 to ca. AD 100). He was of a priestly family, a devoted student, and, at least in the early part of his life, a Pharisee. After visiting Rome in AD 64, he was thoroughly impressed by Roman life. However, he felt compelled to join those in his homeland who wished to rebel against Rome (ca. AD 66). He led Jewish troops in Galilee, where he was accused of treachery. The rebels were defeated by Rome, and he was imprisoned by Vespasian. Because he predicted that Vespasian would become emperor, Josephus was freed in AD 69 when this became a fact. To the end of his life, he was supported by Vespasian and his family. He lived out his days in Rome where he pursued a career of writing. His works are basically a defense of himself, though they also defend Rome and his own people.

Josephus's major works are *The Jewish War,* which covers the history from about 175 BC to AD 66; *Antiquities of the Jews,* which covers Jewish history from creation to AD 66; *Against Apion,* also known as "On the Antiquity of the Jewish People," which is a defense of the Jews, and the *Life* of Josephus, which, along with another minor work, defended his behavior during the Jewish war.

Josephus apparently felt compelled to defend himself and to explain his people to the Romans, as well as explaining the Romans to the Jews. In doing this, he called Judaism a philosophy and its various sects "philosophical trends." Josephus planned to write numerous other works, but even though some other books have at times been credited to him, modern scholarship now concludes that no others exist. They may never have been written.

He referred both to written sources and to oral traditions which he used. Most scholars agree that he generally used his biblical and apocryphal sources with reasonable care. His use of other sources is assumed to be less careful. Regardless, we must never forget that his overriding purposes appear to have been more important to him than accuracy and fairness in the use of his sources.

The Apocrypha

These fourteen books were included in the Septuagint (LXX) version of the Old Testament which was in Greek. They were not included in the Hebrew canon as decided at Jamnia (Jabneh), about AD 90-110. Roman Catholics have accepted them as a part of the Old Testament while most Protestants and Evangelicals do not.

Most of the books of the Apocrypha are of little value as historical sources. However 1 and 2 Maccabees are notable exceptions. First Maccabees deals with the period from about 175-135 BC. It was apparently written to establish the legitimacy of the Hasmonaeans as rulers over Judea and should be understood and evaluated in that light. Second Maccabees claims to be a summary of an earlier, five-volume history by a man of Cyrene named Jason. It does not follow after the material of 1 Maccabees, but parallels it. Further, the evaluation of the Hasmonaeans is much less affirmative in 2 Maccabees. Most scholars generally assess the author of 1 Maccabees to have been a better historian than the author of 2 Maccabees. Suffice it to say here that I agree.

The Dead Sea Scrolls

Since immediately after World War II, a large number of scrolls, fragments, and other written remains have been found at the northwest end of the Dead Sea at and in the vicinity of Qumran and 'Ain Feshkha. The occupation of the ruins can be dated from about 132 BC to about AD 67/68. During this period the region was clearly occupied by Jewish people. Later it was made into a Roman garrison. Finally, there was a brief Jewish reoccupation at the time of the Second Jewish Revolt (AD 132-135).

The numerous documents include large numbers of biblical (Old Testament) materials. However, for our purposes, the actual documents of the sect which lived in these communities reflect the times in which we are interested in our study. The documents which they wrote are sectarian and are concerned with practice and belief, as well as with future hopes. Nothing is actually of the nature of a history, though there are numerous historical allusions.

It is generally concluded that the sect which lived in this region and produced these materials was the Essenes. Using these documents for historical resources must be done with care, always remembering that a specific order of faith and practice was being both propagated and justified. They do add significantly to our knowledge of this part of our period, however.

The Pseudepigrapha

This collection of writings comes from the general period of the second Temple (516 BC-AD 70). The writings are of the same nature as the books of the Apocrypha, but were not included among them. Their title means "the false superscription." The books generally were ascribed to ancient heroes but clearly were not written by them.

The material in this collection of writings is of many kinds. However, nothing like a history of the period we are studying has been identified. Occasional references may add detail to our knowledge of the era. However, they are of far more value in understanding the thought processes of the era than in establishing historical detail.

Philo of Alexandria

A member of the Diaspora, Philo lived in Alexandria in Egypt from about 20 BC to about AD 50. He was without doubt the most significant Jewish philosopher of the era. He was well-educated in Greek thought and philosophy and sought to make Judaism both understandable and palatable to the thinking people of the Roman world. Philo led a Jewish delegation from Alexandria to Rome about AD 40 to plead the cause of Judaism before the Emperor Caligula. In a narrative of that visit, he gave some very detailed information of that era, particularly about Agrippa I who ruled over various parts of Palestine about AD 37-44. Outside of this, occasional other references add small amounts of historical detail to our knowledge of the period.

The Old Testament

The debate continues as to what parts, if any, of the Old Testament are of value for the study of the interbiblical history. Parts of Daniel seem to apply to the period of Antiochus Epiphanes, at least up to 165 BC. This is true whether the book was put in its final form at that time or the author looked ahead through the miracle of inspiration. In addition, some parts of the canon known as The Writings (Hebrew, *Kethubim;* Latin, *Hagiographa*) also seem to give insight into the mood of part of this era. However, as a basic source for our study of the history of the interbiblical period, the Old Testament is not of major significance.

The New Testament

As long as the latter limits of the interbiblical history are as I have defined them, the New Testament is a primary source for approximately the last century of the period. Remembering that while neither the Gospels nor the Book of Acts were written with the primary purposes of giving us a modern history of this period, they do give us significant detail for our study. The Gospels give many details of life in Palestine, while Acts adds to this and then describes other features of history and culture throughout the Diaspora, all the way to Rome. In addition to these sources, the Epistles give occasional historical details.

The Rabbinic Literature

The term Rabbinic Literature is used to designate the large collections of material prepared by the rabbis after the destruction of Jerusalem in AD 70. It includes the Talmuds, the Targums, the Mishna, the Midrashim, and the Tosephta. The Talmuds were collected in both Palestine and Babylon. They include both Mishna and Gemara, the interpretation and application of the Mishna. The Mishna is a collection of laws and regulations which enlarge upon the legal codes of the Old Testament. The Targums are Aramaic translations and/or paraphrases of the Old Testament. Where they are paraphrases, they occasionally add historical detail to our knowledge. The Midrashim are homiletical commentaries on the Old Testament, also giving occasional historical detail and illustrations. The Tosephta (supplement) is similar to the Mishna, including those things which were not included there.

All of these were completed long after the era with which we are concerned, some as much as five or six centuries later. Their historical value is, therefore, not all that great. On the other hand, where they do give historical detail, they must at least be considered.

Greek and Latin Authors

Numerous works of Greek and Latin authors from the interbiblical period survive. However, they were generally unconcerned with the geographical region which is our major focus. On the other hand, some of their allusions must be considered. Their basic value lies in forcing us to see the relations between empire-shaping events and their repercussions in the outlying province of Palestine.

Archaeology

The final source of our knowledge of the era is the excavations of archaeologists in Palestine. These give us occasional manuscript fragments and more often coins reflecting the ruling authorities. Far more importantly, they enable us to see the remains of daily life from the era.

We can begin to deduce what effect the events of national and international significance had upon the people of the land. Rulers gave commands. Common people experienced the consequences. Sometimes when rulers seemed to be shaking the world, ordinary folk seem to have been unaffected. At other times, the decisions of far-distant rulers brought crisis, chaos, and catastrophe as the price which the common people paid.

2
The Rise of Greece

From the fall of Babylon in 539 BC, the region known as the Fertile
Crescent lay under Persian dominion. The empire of Persia ruled over
more territory than any empire which the world had yet known. It was
a gentle dictatorship, bringing an era of peace to the many diverse
peoples over whom it ruled. Among those were the people of Judah with
their capital at Jerusalem. Except that they were not free of foreign
taxation, the Jewish people were probably better off than they had been
in any similar time in their history. Further, except for the fact that they
were not an independent kingdom, the nation of the Jews was probably
as free to do what they pleased as they had ever been, except in the time
of David.

To an outside observer, the world situation in the middle of the fourth
century BC would have looked as if the Persian Empire should have
stood for centuries to come. That view would have been utterly wrong.
By the end of the third quarter of that century, Persia had ceased to exist
as a nation. Further, its once mighty army had been shattered and its
remnants driven forever from its far-flung empire.

The defeat and decimation of Persia had been accomplished by the
conquering forces of Greece. In fact, that defeat had been accomplished
by the personality and military brilliance of one man—Alexander the
Great. His brilliance as a leader is unquestioned. But underlying that
brilliance was a magnificent ideal which motivated him. That ideal had
apparently been implanted in him by his mentor, Aristotle. This ideal
was that the world should be Hellenized.

Hellenism

Hellenism is the term used to describe the process by which Alexander
planned on giving the world one culture, one language, and one way of
life. The culture, the language, and the way of life were all Greek. When
a youth in Macedon, this concept had been woven into the very fiber of

his being through his training. After he succeeded his father to the throne of Macedon, he set forth to make his ideal into a reality.

A Common Culture

Unlike conquerors before him, Alexander was neither motivated by greed for territorial possession nor for personal wealth. He sought to share his glorious culture and language with the rest of humanity. He sought to make all races and cultures believe that they belonged together in "the inhabited world (*oikumene*)," as D. S. Russell so aptly put it. For Alexander the ecumenical movement included not only religion but the totality of life.

Once national boundaries had been destroyed by Alexander's armies, he and his successors set about to establish a common culture. This was done in two ways: the establishment of cities, and the spread of a common language. The *Koine* (common) Greek became the language of the empire. It was the language of business, government, and the common man. This does not mean the average person but rather the ordinary person. (The spread of *Koine* Greek, by the way, made it possible for Paul and the early Christians to be understood wherever they went throughout the Roman Empire.) No matter what a person's native language was, shortly after the conquest by Greece, everyone understood the *Koine*.

The City

To Alexander, because of the nature of his homeland, the secret to any successful government was the city or, more correctly, the city-state. This was the central and properly organized city which provided government, culture, and the opportunity for successful business to all of its citizens. It also provided protection and guaranteed peace. As he moved his armies across the world, Alexander settled large numbers of Greek citizens and discharged soldiers at strategic places where highways met. There his cities were established. However, in the region of Syria-Palestine, he came across a different situation. Cities had already been built at such places. There Alexander generally had only to develop existing cities into the Greek cities of his ideal. In general, that made his goal of acculturization easier. However, when he came to Jerusalem, that process created major problems for his followers.

As a further part of his process of acculturization, gymnasiums were established in the cities which had been created as centers of Greek civilization. The Greeks placed a major emphasis upon the beauty of the human form. In every Greek city gymnasiums provided a place for young people to exercise and perform in the nude. Further, these gymnasiums served as the social centers of the city. There Greek ideals, such as patriotism and loyalty to one's nation and companions, were taught. Sadly, however, in other instances they served as the center for sexual perversions and gross licentiousness.

The cities of Alexander also served as centers for business, government, and intellectual discussions. Such were usually held at the *agora*, the public marketplace. Here matters of state and commerce as well as matters of philosophy and conscience were settled. Later at the *agora*, Christian missionaries proclaimed their faith and found hearers willing to listen and consider what they said.

Greek society was generally prosperous, at least so far as the Greek cities were concerned. Thus, the people, at least the citizens, had time for amusements. These in general involved athletic contests and chariot races. These amusements required that each Greek city have a stadium and a hippodrome. After a gymnasium, these two were the most important outward signs of a Hellenized city. At the same time, the cities also furnished entertainment of a more intellectual nature through the theater. However, the local dramas of the provinces of the empire left something to be desired when contrasted with the classical Greek dramas. Many of the Greek dramas imported were quite licentious. At its best, however, the Greek theaters built into the hillsides outside of a city brought the best of Greek literary heritage to the scattered cities of the empire.

Literature

The coming of the Greek literature made other impacts upon the new cities and the old cities in Greece's new territories. All of these ancient lands and peoples already had long literary traditions. Under the influence of Hellenization, the new generations believed that thought must be Greek thought and that literature must be Greek literature. As an outgrowth of this, much of the ancient literatures of the conquered lands was translated into Greek. This impetus caused the Old Testament to be translated into the Greek Septuagint (LXX). It was also the driving force that caused a man like Philo of Alexandria to write to the world about Judaism in terms of Greek philosophical thought. The LXX gave the early Christians a Scripture which could be understood worldwide from which to proclaim Jesus. The work of Philo had made the basis of their proclamation respectable in the intellectual centers of the ancient world.

That also opened doors of opportunity which would not otherwise have been available.

Religion

In the ancient world of the Orient, people commonly believed that the gods and the culture of a conquering people had to be superior to those of the conquered people. Israel alone had developed a theology of conquest, which said that their defeats could be evidence for the sovereignty of their God who used such as instruments of punishment and judgment. However, even though this was proclaimed in such books as Jeremiah, Ezekiel, and Isaiah 40—66, it was still not grasped by a multitude of the Jewish people. To many of them, the victories of Greece indicated the superiority of Greek ways. This led to a desire to assimilate the Greek ways. Furthermore, the Greeks who were settled into the new Hellenic cities became the leaders of those cities by nature of their citizenship. That, too, made their ways desirable to many people. Thus many influential Jewish people sought to become fully Hellenized. This meant participating in all affairs of the cities, including the gymnasiums. But this created the biggest problem for the Jews. Circumcision was derided by the Greeks as a defilement of the body. In order to be able to appear naked in the gymnasiums without being ridiculed or ostracized, Hellenized Jews sometimes had an operation performed which made it appear that they had never been circumcised. This was considered by the orthodox to be a denial of their covenant commitments and of their racial and religious identity.

Greek cities provided for the worship of many gods. This allowed the Jews of the Diasopra the freedom to worship the God of Israel in their own way. To that extent, the policy was beneficial to Judaism. On the other hand, in attempting to make Jerusalem a Greek city, such pagan worship created an impossible situation for the orthodox Jews. The worship of other gods could not be permitted.

These two conditions created a tragic and critical situation for the Jews of Jerusalem. Some sought to become Hellenized and others sought to resist the Hellenistic influence to the bitter end. The people in the city struggled against one another—Jew against Jew. The very nature of this conflict was hard for the successors of Alexander to understand. They could not comprehend why all of the people could not go along with the policies of Hellenization which some of the people supported so readily. This was even more difficult to understand when those who did go along with Greek policies were generally the leaders of Jerusalem, the wealthy and the influential people of power. The military conquests of Alexander and his successors did not give the Hebrews problems. To the contrary, they had been conquered often enough to be able to endure that. What created the biggest problem for them was Alexander's Hellenizing ideal, the ideal which had sent him forth in the first place. This one feature, more than anything else, holds the key for understanding the crises of at least the early interbiblical period.

Chronological Table

Alexander's Campaigns (333-323 BC)
> Battle of Issus (333 BC)
> Tyre captured (332 BC)
> Gaza captured (332 BC)
> Alexandria founded (331 BC)
> Battle of Gaugamela (331 BC)

Struggles of the Diadochi (323-301 BC)
> Surreptitious conflict (323-ca. 315 BC)
> Ptolemy I controls Egypt (323-283 BC)
> Antigonus Monophthalmos seizes Palestine (ca. 320 BC)
> Ptolemy invades Jerusalem (312 BC)
> Seleucus I captures Babylon (312 BC)
> Antigonus recaptures Palestine (312 BC)
> Battle of Ipsus (302 BC)
> Ptolemy controls Palestine (301 BC)

Alexander's Campaigns (333-323 BC)

On several occasions, the empire of Persia had sought to extend its territory to the west in order to include the city-states of Greece. Each time those highly independent Greek states united in an effort to drive off a common enemy. Although Athens was put to the torch early in the fifth century BC, the Persian attacks were ultimately in every instance unsuccessful.

Some Greek city-states across the Aegean Sea, however, were under Persian domination. After the repeated successful defenses of their homeland, the city-states of Greece proper set forth to liberate their compatriots across the sea. They were relatively unsuccessful, however, due to their intense independence. Though they had been united in defending their homeland, they were not able to collaborate effectively in offensive actions.

These ongoing conflicts, however, did reveal that Persia, for all of its wealth and extensive territorial control, was not as powerful as it appeared. It was an overripe plum, ready for the picking, when any powerful, united enemy might choose to do so.

That time came with the work of Philip of Macedon, father of Alexander. He set forth to unite the people of Thrace, Macedonia, and Ionia. Combining both diplomacy and military confrontation, Philip did what no one before him had done: He united the fiercely independent city-states of Greece. From this foundation, he planned to set forth against the empire of Persia. This plan was thwarted by the assassination of Philip in 336 BC.

Purpose

At this point, Alexander stepped upon the scene. Alexander was a genius in every sense. He was only thirteen when he studied under Aristotle. He was a victorious general in his father's army at eighteen. Upon his father's death, he ascended the throne at the age of twenty. Some of the leaders of the recently subdued city-states thought him too young to rule over them and sought to reestablish their independence. Within two years he demonstrated his political, diplomatic, military, and administrative skills and was in firm control of his father's kingdom. He then set forth on the journey of conquest from which he never returned.

At times Alexander was almost a mystic, particularly as he related to the Greek heritage. He crossed the narrows of the Hellespont and paused at Troy to ponder Greece's ancient glories. Shortly thereafter he fought and defeated a Persian army at the river Granicus. His army swept across Asia Minor, moving as rapidly in advance as the Persians fled in defeat. He was confronted by them again at Issus. There he overwhelmingly defeated them in 333 BC. The fate of Persia was settled at that point for all practical purposes. Most historians date the end of the Persian Empire and the beginning of the Greek Empire at the Greek victory at Issus.

Southern Conquest

Following the victory at Issus, two major routes lay open before Alexander. He was forced to choose. The remnants of the shattered Persian army were retreating eastward. Alexander, however, turned southward into Syria-Palestine, where he expected little or no major opposition. That view, however, was not totally accurate.

Alexander's forces were held up in the southern advance by the Phoenician city of Tyre. Tyre was on an island just off the coastal plain. It held out against his siege for seven months, falling in July, 332 BC. He captured it by building a causeway from the mainland. The magnitude of this victory can perhaps be better understood when we consider that Tyre withstood Nebuchadnezzar for thirteen years. Alexander did not like being slowed down, however, so he wreaked a massive vengeance on the city.

Following that victory, he marched on southward. At this point, his only possible contacts with the Hebrew people may have occurred. The petty states along Alexander's march all were submissive to his suzerainty. Samaria had apparently sent troops to his aid during the siege of Tyre, pledging loyalty to the young ruler.

Josephus reported a visit of Alexander to Jerusalem to offer sacrifice in the Temple. The account reads more like legend than history. It is unlikely that he would have turned aside from his major advance for such a purpose. On the one hand, Alexander's religious tolerance and his desire to have the favor of all the gods would not make such a sacrifice improbable if he had visited Jerusalem. On the other hand, the Talmud records a meeting between the high priest of Jerusalem and Alexander at a site in the Philistine coastal plain. This is quite likely, for such a meeting would have offered an opportunity for the ruler of a small vassal nation to pledge allegiance to the new ruler. Yet, even this narrative has a problem, for the high priest named in the account did not serve until almost a century after Alexander's death. The story may have a basis in fact with the wrong name having become part of the later tradition.

Alexander moved on southward, where the way into Egypt was blocked by the fortress city of Gaza. This city was finally captured in 332 BC, after a two-months' siege. Following its conquest, the way into Egypt lay open. Alexander overcame Egypt with no difficulty. The great city of Alexandria was founded there in 331 BC. It exists to this day, memorializing the genius of this youth from Macedon.

At about this time, the people of Samaria apparently rebelled and burned Alexander's governor alive. No plausible reason for this is known. Alexander set forth on a punitive expedition. He overthrew the people, removed many inhabitants, and settled many Macedonians there. Shechem and a temple on Mount Gerizim were apparently rebuilt afterward. Archaeological evidence appears to verify some kind of military campaign in the region along with a resettlement of Shechem about 330 BC. The building of the temple on Gerizim and the intermarriage following the settlement of the Macedonians intensified the problems between the people of Jerusalem and those of Samaria that continued throughout the New Testament era.

Eastern Conquest

Following the brief campaign in Samaria, Alexander and his forces marched northward and then turned eastward. During the time of Alexander's Palestinian and Egyptian campaigns, the Persian army had been given an opportunity to regroup. The Greek armies crossed the Euphrates and the Tigris and in October of 331 BC met and defeated the Persian forces at Gaugamela, on the plains east of the Tigris. This defeat brought the Persian Empire to its ultimate end. King Darius III fled, abandoning his family and wealth. He was assassinated by one of his satraps in the following year. The family and wealth of Darius III fell into Alexander's hands after the victory of Gaugamela.

Alexander hardly paused after this victory. The capitals of Persia fell to him one by one: Susa, Ecbatana, and, finally, Perseopolis. At Perseopolis, Alexander performed a very uncharacteristic act of vengeance for Persia's having burned Athens about a hundred and fifty years earlier: He utterly destroyed the city.

The army of Alexander continued its eastward march. It crossed the Indus River, having moved through Afghanistan, India, and ultimately into the region now known as West Pakistan. At this point, Alexander's troops decided they had gained enough glory, attained enough wealth, and been away from home long enough. Alexander turned homeward.

The Greek king's vision of one world and one culture had been essentially achieved. He did not treat conquered peoples as captives or serfs. He encouraged intermarriage with the conquered people, and took Scythian and Persian wives for himself. On his way home, Alexander caught a fever (generally assumed to have been malaria) in Babylon. There he died in 323 BC.

He left a mighty legacy. To his successors was given the largest empire the world had ever known. To the Western world, he left a culture which still shapes our lives. To the Christian missionaries yet to come, he left a language by which their message could easily be spread to the ends of the earth.

The Struggle for Palestine (323-301 BC)

From the standpoint of the Greek Empire, the struggle for Palestine was not the main issue in the period following the death of Alexander. The major issue was the struggle for succession to the throne of and authority of Alexander. This has been referred to by some as the period of the Diadochi (the "successors"). Alexander's death at such a young age was wholly unexpected, thus no provision had been made for how his succession was to be handled.

The Legal Heirs

No single outstanding successor to Alexander was on the scene when he died. The only immediately legal heir to the throne of Macedonia was Alexander's half-brother Philip Arrhidaeus, who was also reportedly half-witted. Such a claim may have been made by nonlegal claimants simply to discredit him. However, the facts appear to support this claim.

Further, at the time of Alexander's death, his wife Roxana (a Scythian) was pregnant. She later gave birth to a son who was named Alexander after his father. This child was immediately accepted, outwardly at least, as Alexander's legal heir. Obviously, however, he could not have reigned for many years to come.

The Diadochi

A self-appointed council of seven of Alexander's leading generals sat to decide the fate of the empire. One of their number, Perdiccas, who was probably the oldest, was appointed guardian of the legitimate heirs. The other six divided the empire among themselves, each serving as regents for the legal heirs. For our purposes, only three of these are of significance. Antigonus was probably at the time of this division the more powerful and astute of the generals. He was appointed governor over Asia Minor. Ptolemy, probably the second most powerful, was assigned Egypt. Antipater, the third most significant in terms of generalship and probably the ablest administrator was appointed regent over Macedonia and Greece.

In 321 BC a coalition of Alexander's successors arranged for the assassination of the guardian, Perdiccas. He had become feared because of an open alliance which he had made with Alexander's mother (Olympias) and his widow (Roxana). This had given rise to the suspicion, perhaps justified, that he was seeking supreme authority for himself. Following Perdiccas's death, Antipater was named guardian, but he died in 318 BC. He was succeeded by his son, Cassander. At this time civil war broke out in Macedonia and Greece, so his attentions were directed there.

Shortly thereafter, perhaps as a part of that civil war, Alexander's half-brother was murdered by Alexander's mother. This was an apparent attempt to assure that her grandson would ultimately ascend the throne. In retaliation, Cassander put Olympias to death and then quickly executed both Alexander's wife Roxana and his son. Following these events, no legal heir to the throne of Alexander remained alive. The facade of regency and guardianship had been stripped away, and conflict and intrigue in the struggle for succession became open to public display. The date by which this was effected is a bit unclear. It was possibly as early as 317 BC and had certainly been done by 315 BC. From this time, we can focus our attention wholly upon the developments as they directly affected Palestine.

Before proceeding further, we need to clarify some geographical terms used of the region about which we are concerned. Many writers, both ancient and modern, use the term *Coele-Syria*. Other writers, more generally modern ones, use as a synonymous term the expression *Syria and Palestine*. Still others limit themselves simply to *Palestine*. This is what I intend to do. As used in this book, this term (along with all of the others) refers to the whole of the land bridge from the Mediterranean on the west to the Transjordan plateau on the east, and from the wilderness on the south to and including the territory of Phoenicia and part of Syria on the north.

After the struggle to seize control of Alexander's empire moved into the open, Palestine became the focus of a major series of conflicts. Ptolemy I, also known as Ptolemy Lagi and as Ptolemy Soter, sought to secure his control of Egypt. He founded a dynasty which lasted until about 30 BC. Ptolemy recognized, as Egyptian rulers had for centuries before him, that the key to security in Egypt rested with the control of Palestine. When Palestine was controlled by Egypt, no significant threat could be made to a strong ruler in that land. About 320 BC, he sent an army into Palestine and briefly seized control of the region.

In the meantime, Antigonus, ruler of Asia Minor, sought to gain control of Babylon, which had been assigned to a general named Seleucus. Antigonus defeated his opponent, who fled to Egypt, seeking and finding sanctuary from Ptolemy. Ptolemy appointed Seleucus as one of his military commanders. Antigonus, in the meantime, turned his attention toward Palestine. His armies marched southward, attacking and defeating major and minor cities all the way to and including Gaza. Sometime during these conflicts, Antigonus apparently lost an eye in battle, for he came to be known as Antigonus Monophthalmos ("the one-eyed").

Problems in Asia Minor, however, forced Antigonus to withdraw. When he did, he left Palestine under the control of his son, Demetrius. Ptolemy and Seleucus seized this opportunity to renew their attempt to control Palestine. In their initial attack upon Gaza, 312 BC, Demetrius was defeated. This allowed Ptolemy to regain control over Palestine and allowed Seleucus to march on to Babylon.

At this point, Ptolemy invaded Jerusalem. He had discovered that the Jews would not fight on the sabbath, so he marched into the city unopposed. One ancient record says that he carried away one hundred thousand captives. Given what we know of the exaggerated claims of ancient conquerors and what we know of conditions in Egypt shortly thereafter, that number is probably too large. However, Ptolemy's conquest of Jerusalem and his carrying away a significant number of captives as slaves and hostages is unquestioned. We do have numerous evidences that Ptolemy settled Jews in various cities throughout his kingdom during that period. However, the large settlements in Alexandria and Elephantine probably predate this era.

Seleucus in the meantime marched toward Babylon. He captured that city in the latter part of 312 BC. At that point, he established a dynasty which endured until about 56 BC. This feat marked the end of the friendship between Ptolemy and Seleucus and the beginning of their bitter rivalry. This rivalry continued among their successors until the end of their dynasties.

Ptolemy's control of Palestine was brief. Antigonus, having gained control of the situation in Asia Minor, invaded Palestine less than six months after Ptolemy's victory at Gaza. Once again, Antigonus' successful advance left Ptolemy with no alternative but to retreat to Egypt.

For about a decade, these were the conditions in Palestine. The struggle for control of the empire continued, but in other theaters of action. About 302 BC, however, the situation changed.

The Battle of Ipsus

Seleucus organized a coalition to attack Antigonus. Seleucus was to come from the east, two other generals from the west and north, and Ptolemy from the south. The result of this concerted attack was twofold. First, Ptolemy held his forces back. The battle was joined by the others at Ipsus in Phrygia, and Antigonus was defeated, dying during the course of the battle. His kingdom was divided among the three victorious generals. It had been decided in advance that his territory would be divided four ways, with Palestine being assigned to Ptolemy. However, since Ptolemy did not show up, Palestine was assigned to Seleucus instead.

The second result of the Battle of Ipsus brought an immediate problem to Palestine. While the three allies had been defeating Antigonus, Ptolemy had been taking advantage of the situation. He simply marched his armies into Palestine and took control. This certainly created a critical situation. Ptolemy controlled Palestine, and Seleucus claimed it. While this obviously aroused the wrath of Seleucus, his forces were too weakened by the battle for him to do anything about it.

For slightly more than a century, Ptolemy and his successors were able to maintain their control of Palestine proper. However, Seleucus did hold onto the territory of Syria. In fact, he established his capital at Antioch.

During the approximately twenty-year period in which the struggle for the control of Palestine had gone on, this territory was the scene of frequent battles. Ptolemy's armies marched through the region at least three times, and Antigonus's armies came twice. Almost certainly, the people of Jerusalem were divided in their support of one or the other. We do know that some Jews had served in the army of Alexander. It is likely that they did so in the armies of his successors. Further, a high priest of the era apparently was a supporter of Ptolemy and had to flee for safety during one of the invasions of Antigonus. At the very least, the era was a time of uncertainty and chaos for the people of Judea. At the very most, they would have been almost constantly involved in conflict of one kind or another.

The Samaritans

Most people are aware of the antipathy which Samaritans and Jews had for each other during the time of the New Testament. We do not know all of the reasons for this, for the issue is quite involved. It possibly goes back into the era of the divided kingdoms. Since the later people of Judea were the descendants of the southerners, their dislike of the people of Samaria may go all the way back to the conflicts between the two kingdoms. This is particularly possible since during that era the Northern Kingdom whose capital was Samaria for part of the time, was generally victorious over the Southern Kingdom.

Following the defeat of the Northern Kingdom by Assyria in 722/21 BC, numerous Jews were deported from the north, including Samaria, and numerous Assyrian captives from other nations were settled there. We can assume that with the passage of time intermarriage took place. This would make the people of Samaria a source of dislike to the Jews of Jerusalem. This was clearly the case during the period after the return of the Hebrews from the Babylonian Exile in 539 BC, and later. We are certainly aware of ongoing conflict and disagreement between the two peoples throughout this period (cf. Ezra. 4:1-3, 8-23; 5:3 to 6:13; Neh. 4; 6; 13:23-28).

These things, however, were even more focalized during the period we have been considering. Alexander's settlement of Macedonians in the region of Samaria increased the problems of intermarriage. Further, the building of a separate temple at Gerizim accelerated the deteriorating relations. During this time, the Samaritans established their own canon of the Scriptures, which included the Pentateuch and a very long and enlarged version of Joshua. The events of these three decades (333 BC-301 BC) solidified the process which had been going on for almost four centuries. The end result was that two peoples who were deeply related and had much in common became the bitterest of enemies.

3

The Rule of the Ptolemies Over Palestine

(301-198 BC)

For our purposes, the ultimate result of the defeat of Antigonus at the Battle of Ipsus was Ptolemaic control of Palestine. As noted in the preceding chapter, while Seleucus was winning at Ipsus and afterward being assigned authority over Palestine, Ptolemy had marched into the land and actually taken control. The legal claim to Palestine which Seleucus had been given was quite good. But the actual military occupation of the land was even better, insofar as genuine control went. Further, the control of Palestine by Ptolemy and his successors brought a time of peace to the land of the Jews: Jerusalem and Judea. From their standpoint, if from no other, Ptolemaic rule meant a time of stability and security. In general, they were able to pursue their own affairs in quietness.

Chronological Table
The Ptolemaic Era (301-198 BC)

Egypt	Syria	High Priests
Ptolemy I Soter (323-283)	Seleucus I (312-281)	Onias I Simeon I Eleazar
Ptolemy II Philadelphus (283-246)	Antiochus I (281/280-261)	Manasseh
	First Syrian War (274-272)	
	Antiochus II (261-246)	Onias II
	Second Syrian War (260-252)	(Joseph the Tobiad)

Ptolemy III Euergetes (246-221)	Seleucus II (246-226)	
	Third Syrian War (246-241)	
	Seleucus III (226-223)	
Ptolemy IV Philopator (221-204)	Antiochus III (223-187)	Simeon II (220-190)
	Fourth Syrian War (221-217)	
Ptolemy V Epiphanes (204-180)		
	Fifth Syrian War (201-198)	

The Rise of Egypt (301-246 BC)

Ptolemy I Soter

When Ptolemy arrived in Egypt in 323 BC, he came as one of several rulers controlling various parts of Alexander's kingdom as regents. They were actually called by a Persian administrative designation, *satrap*. For all practical purposes, however, Ptolemy I ruled as a king and about 305 BC had himself actually designated king. So successful was he that all of the male sovereigns of this dynasty bore the throne name of Ptolemy.

Upon his arrival in Egypt, Ptolemy I Soter (or "savior," as he was called) set about to establish his rule as a continuation of the pattern established by the pharaohs. This worked to his benefit and that of his successors in a variety of ways. First, the pharaohs had been worshiped as divine. Such adoration undergirded the Ptolemies's authority and power in ways which none of Alexander's other successors experienced. Further, for over a millenium, the pharaohs had enjoyed the position of owning all of the land of Egypt. Parts were leased out to temples and wealthy tenants. The rest was farmed by serfs under the overseers of the pharaoh. This added to the wealth of the king. All trade was under the control of the pharaoh. As a result, wealth poured into the treasuries of Ptolemy I.

In addition, once Ptolemy's control of Palestine was assured, Egypt enjoyed a time of peace which meant that national resources did not have to be expended in war. The control of the coasts of Egypt and Palestine, as well as of Cyprus which was regarded as a part of this region, brought even more resources from trade into the palace of the king of Egypt. Furthermore, the defeat of the people of Petra in the southern Transjordan by his son, Ptolemy II, brought the last trade route in the land bridge of Palestine under Egyptian control. The end result was even more wealth and prosperity. Ptolemy I made Alexandria his capital and built it into one of the more magnificent cities of the world. The citizens of Alexandria enjoyed wealth and prosperity generally unknown in the ancient world. The Jewish Diaspora located there became one of the more significant if not the most significant centers of Judaism outside of Jerusalem. Because of their wealth and significance, the LXX was produced, giving them, as well as other Greek-speaking Jews, their Scriptures in their own language.

Needless to say, the wealth and power of Ptolemy I put him in a position to be envied by all of the other successors of Alexander. He and his descendants were among the wealthiest and most powerful rulers in the world during the third century BC. With the resources at his command, an ordinary man could have wielded extraordinary power. Ptolemy I was no ordinary man. With his resources, he built an extraordinary kingdom which became a major power base that endured for the greater part of the second century BC.

Ptolemy II Philadelphus

With the death of Ptolemy I in 283 BC, Ptolemy II, otherwise known as Philadelphus, succeeded to the throne of Egypt. Two years later, Seleucus was murdered (281 BC) and was succeeded by his son Antiochus I, in 281/80 BC. The history of this era is not wholly clear, but the First Syrian War broke out between Egypt and Syria about 275/74 BC when Ptolemy II invaded Syria. The war lasted for three to four years with no overwhelming victory for either side. Apparently the land side of the battle was generally controlled by Antiochus I and the naval side was generally dominated by Ptolemy Philadelphus. The war drew to a close about 272 BC. Although Ptolemy had been unable to expand his territory, he had been able to maintain all of his territorial claims against the forces of Antiochus.

A decade of peace ensued until the death of Antiochus I (261 BC). He was succeeded by Antiochus II who immediately sought to reassert the Seleucid claims over the territory of Palestine. He attacked the forces of Ptolemy II in 260 BC and the Second Syrian War began. Almost nothing is known of this conflict. It was wholly indecisive, for when peace was concluded in 253/52 BC, the territorial boundaries were just as they were when the conflict had erupted. The basis of the peace was the establishment of a covenant between the two kingdoms. This was sealed by the giving of Ptolemy II's daughter, Berenice, to Antiochus II in marriage. For the remaining six years of his reign, Ptolemy Philadelphus ruled in peace. His reign had been the high point of the kingdom of the Ptolemies. Wealth, power, and prominence were all characteristic of this time. The images of luxurious despotism in Oriental kingdoms which most people hold in their imaginations were all true in the court of Ptolemy II Philadelphus. Unfortunately for his successors, it did not last long.

The Decline of Egypt (246-198 BC)

The marriage of Berenice to Antiochus II, which had brought peace in 252 BC was also the source of the return of war in 246/45 BC. In order to marry the princess from Alexandria, Antiochus had been forced to divorce his first wife, Laodice. This also included removing her son Seleucus from the line of succession. Both acts were to be the source of future trouble in the Syrian kingdom. In the meantime, Antiochus II and his new queen, Berenice, had a son.

Laodice had loyal followers at the court of Syria, however. In 246 BC she was able to have her former husband, Antiochus II, poisoned. Then, in order to prevent Berenice's son from ascending the throne under a guardianship, Laodice's followers murdered Berenice and her son. This paved the way for Laodice's son to ascend the throne of the Seleucid empire as Seleucus II.

Ptolemy III Euergetes

In the meantime, Ptolemy II died in Alexandria. He was followed on the throne of Egypt by his son, Ptolemy III Euergetes. He is sometimes referred to as Euergetes I, because Ptolemy VIII was also named Euergetes and is thus referred to as Euergetes II. For our purposes here, since they have different numbers after the Ptolemy, I see no reason to further complicate matters by adding a second number to the name.

The murder of Berenice in Antioch would have been an affront to the Egyptian kings at any time, for she had been an Egyptian princess. She was actually the sister of Ptolemy III, so he was especially bent on avenging her death and the death of her son. With speed and energy, Ptolemy III invaded the territory of Syria in the Third Syrian War, also called the Laodicean War. Again, we know very little of the details of this conflict. It lasted from about 246 to 241 BC and was clearly the most significant military victory any Ptolemaic king ever won. He captured Damascus, penetrated far into the Syrian kingdom, took large amounts of booty, and could have proceeded further. However, he was called home to Egypt, opening the door for Seleucus II to recapture much of his lost territory, including Damascus. In spite of his best efforts, the Syrian king was unable to move his forces into the Egyptian parts of Palestine. A battle did take place between the opposing armies somewhere in Palestine, but the exact location is unknown. Seleucus II was defeated and had to return home hurriedly. Once again, peace was concluded, leaving the final territorial boundaries essentially where they were at the outset.

Ptolemy IV Philopator

For the next ten to fifteen years, peace ruled over this region as the center of international activity turned to Asia. This left Palestine in relative quiet. Seleucus II died in 226 BC and was succeeded on the throne of Syria by his son, Seleucus III. He reigned briefly from 226 to 223 BC, when he was killed by poison, apparently at the instigation of his younger brother who followed him upon the throne as Antiochus III, later known as Antiochus the Great. He was only twenty at the time.

Shortly thereafter, Ptolemy III died in Egypt and was succeeded by his son, Ptolemy IV Philopator. He, too, was quite young, being seventeen upon his accession. A totally inept ruler, he was more concerned with art and religion than with war and government. He preferred to delegate such matters to others and assigned the responsibilities to people even more inept than himself.

In contrast, Antiochus III was quite capable. He first consolidated his authority at home by eliminating any rivals to the throne and then set forth to regain the Seleucid territory (as he viewed it) of Syria and Palestine. This began the Fourth Syrian War in 221 BC. Antiochus marched successfully down the coast, capturing or accepting the surrender of city after city, until he had marched all the way to Raphia on the Egyptian frontier. There the Syrian forces were met in 217 BC by a reorganized Egyptian army and were overwhelmingly defeated. Antiochus III raced home. The Egyptians, almost at their leisure, retook all the territory of Palestine which Antiochus had seized in his advance. Thus, the Fourth Syrian War came to an end with the territorial boundaries still essentially unchanged. But the winds of change were blowing.

Ptolemy V Epiphanes

The affairs of state and empire kept the attention of Antiochus the Great for a number of years. But he never forgot his claims to Palestine. However, Ptolemy IV died in 204/03 BC and was succeeded to the throne by his four-year-old son, Ptolemy V Epiphanes. This led to the rise of numerous rival claimants to the throne and offered Antiochus the opportunity for which he had been looking. His campaigns in the east had been brought to a successful conclusion about 204 BC.

In 202 BC, Antiochus began a campaign which was aborted for some unknown reason. However, in 201 BC he marched in earnest, beginning the Fifth Syrian War. (It was also the last Syrian war.) Several victories were enjoyed by Antiochus, but the overthrow of the Egyptians forces in 200 BC brought a final end to the major campaigns. All that was left was the mopping up. By 198 BC, all of Syria and Palestine yielded allegiance to Antiochus III, who had earned the title, "the Great." At long last, the territory which had been given to the Seleucids following the battle of Ipsus was under their control. Egyptian hegemony over Palestine was gone forever.

The Hebrews Under the Ptolemies

In general, we know very few specifics about conditions in Jerusalem and Judea during the period of Ptolemaic rule in Palestine. However, we can deduce a fair amount from evidence gleaned from a number of different sources.

Administration

Politically, it is almost certain that the region of Palestine would have been administered through a military governor called a *strategos* who was probably based at Ptolemais. Whether other Egyptian or Greek officials were scattered throughout the region or whether each local province supplied its own native authorities who were responsible to the *strategos,* we do not know.

Admittedly arguments from silence are suspect, but since no mention is made of such foreign officials either in Josephus or in the rabbinic materials, we can probably assume that the high priest and Sanhedrin administered local affairs. Tax-collectors were most likely Hebrews. The Ptolemaic empire generally used "tax farmers" for the collection of taxes. They were among the ancient world's most successful tax gatherers. The tax farmers assembled at Alexandria periodically where they bid at tax auctions for the right to collect taxes in a particular region or district.

Josephus recorded the story of one such tax farmer, Joseph the Tobiad. He was a citizen of Jerusalem and was related to the high priest Onias. Joseph won the right to collect taxes in Palestine and entered the region with two thousand Ptolemaic soldiers at his disposal. He so abused the people that they paid his heavy taxes with speed. He maintained his position for over twenty years. During this period he also became extremely wealthy from his profits through overtaxing. Josephus gave some indication that the high priest may also have paid the Ptolemies for the privilege of serving, though this is not certain.

Economically the Hebrew people seemed to have fared fairly well during this period. They paid rather high taxes to the Egyptian kingdom, even if the figures of Josephus are considered to be exaggerated on the high side. The very fact that they were prosperous enough to pay even a portion of such taxes indicates a relative degree of economic success.

War and Peace

During the century when Jerusalem and its environs were under Ptolemaic rule, five Syrian wars were fought. This involved a significant number of troops moving to and fro throughout the land. It also involved a large number of battles fought on Palestinian soil. However, as noted, these troops usually moved on the coastal road and the major battles were fought over coastal cities. Jerusalem, sitting astride the highway of the central highlands appears to have been spared much of the burden of these wars. Yet on some occasions, troops actually moved into Jerusalem and carried captives into Egypt. On the other hand, the Jews in Alexandria enjoyed a great deal of peace and prosperity, a condition which would not have been likely if the people of their homeland had created too many problems for the Ptolemaic rulers. Further, a number of Jews also appear to have served in the armies of Egypt. That, too, would not have been too likely if they had viewed the Egyptian armies to have been their great enemy.

Josephus also recorded, in a story which may be suspect, that Ptolemy III went to Jerusalem to offer sacrifices following the Third Syrian War. While the story itself may not be true, it at least reflects a relationship which was far from inimical. It is more likely that Ptolemy sent sacrifices to be offered than that he went himself, although that is not impossible.

Hellenization

There is no way of knowing how much the policy of Hellenization originated by Alexander was carried on among the Jews in this period. We do know that the Ptolemies carried on this policy less aggressively than other successors to Alexander in the other parts of the empire. Also, it appears to have been administered less aggressively in the provinces than in the land of Egypt itself. Further, the Jews were very strict sabbath observers during this period. Though this is arguing from silence, the laxity in sabbath observance that accompanied the acceptance of Hellenizing policies in other eras makes it likely that such policies were not strictly enforced during these days. Since no mention is made of such enforcement in the typically Hebrew sources related to this period, more than likely the Hellenizing influences were relatively minor, even if they were not nonexistent.

Literary Activity

Perhaps the most significant indication of the conditions under which the Jews lived during this period is the fact that it was a time of significant literary activity. The Old Testament canon of the prophets was completed during this period. Other books of the Bible were brought into final form or were accepted as authoritative. Further, numerous noncanonical books were written by the Hebrews. This kind of literary activity presupposes a time of peace with an opportunity for reflection. In Alexandria itself, the first steps were taken toward the production of the LXX.

Prosperity

All in all, the best evidence we can glean makes it appear that the Jewish state prospered under the rule of the Ptolemies. If it did not prosper, it at least does not seem to have suffered as it had done at other periods of its history. It also appears to have been relatively free from foreign domination or interference, being allowed pretty much to do its own thing in its own way. Foreign taxes were a burden, but were nothing new. The Jews had paid foreign taxes for centuries in one form or another. At the same time, the people of Jerusalem were quite aware that they were under foreign authority. Like other people both before and after them, they longed for independence. Further, if that were not possible to attain, they longed for a ruler who would at least make conditions better rather than worse.

Therefore, when at the end of the Fifth Syrian War it was obvious that the Seleucids had finally defeated the Ptolemies and had wrested control of Palestine from them, this was welcomed by the Jews. They hoped it would be a change for the better. Some, if not all, of the Jewish leaders were quite ready and eager to assert their allegiance to Antiochus III. He had driven the Egyptian soldiers from their territory. The Jewish leaders had been assured that they would have the same degree of independence under him that they had enjoyed before. Further, and more importantly, Antiochus also initially reduced the taxes which the Hebrews and their Temple would be required to pay.

Thus, with a great deal of eagerness, the Sanhedrin, or at least part of it, went forth to meet Antiochus as he approached their city. What the Hebrew leaders did not recognize, or at least did not admit, was that it was to the advantage of Antiochus to improve conditions until he had won their allegiance. They ignored the fact that he could change his policies after he was thoroughly in control. The Jewish leaders may even have deluded themselves into thinking that they were more important to Antiochus III than they were. They greeted him with hope and with cries of joy. All too soon those cries had turned to silence. Eventually, they were transformed into cries of grief and anger. They had hoped things would be better. In the end, things were worse, far worse.

4
The Rule of the Seleucids
(198-ca. 167 BC)

Once again we must deal with the fact that the boundaries between different eras of history are not nearly as clear-cut or well-defined as we might wish. No real question exists as to when this period begins. The final end of Ptolemaic authority and the beginning of Seleucid rule in Palestine is to be dated in 198 BC. The end of the Seleucid rule, however, could be legitimately dated (as various historians do) in 167, 165, 164, or 162 BC. For this reason, I have chosen to be less precise in my delineation and simply say it concluded about 167 BC.

In investigating the historical events of this era, we have more data available than for any preceding period we have considered. However, scholars are relatively certain that 1 Maccabees was used by Josephus and the author of 2 Maccabees. Thus the fact that all three sources record the same event cannot be equated with three separate witnesses to it. We have to be especially careful in evaluating and assimilating the information which our sources give us.

Finally, in seeking both to cover and to understand the events of this period, we shall be forced to backtrack on occasion to approach the same event from several different directions.

Chronological Table
The Seleucid Era (198-167 BC.)

Egypt	Syria	High Priests
Ptolemy V Epiphanes (204-181)	Antiochus III— the Great (223-187)	Simeon II (220-190)
	Conquers Greek cities (193)	
	Driven from Greece (192)	Onias III (190-174)

	Defeated by Rome (188)	
	(Peace of Apamea)	(Conflict with Simon, Temple captain)
Ptolemy VI (181-145)	Seleucus IV Philopator (187-175)	
	Antiochus IV Epiphanes (175-164)	Jason (175-172)
	(Antiochus's Egyptian campaigns, 169-168)	Menelaus (172-162)
		(Judas Maccabeus 167-161)

The Political Situation

Antiochus III the Great

The victory of Antiochus III ("the Great") over Ptolemy V of Egypt brought an end to the Fifth Syrian War (202-198 BC). It also brought to fruition the century-old goal of the Seleucids to control the region of Palestine and Phoenicia which had been assigned to them following their victory of the Battle of Ipsus (302 BC; cf. Ch. 2). However, it did not bring an end to the political and territorial ambitions of Antiochus. He had earlier entered into a treaty with Philip V of Macedon to capture and divide all the territories controlled by Egypt outside of Egypt itself. This included much of Asia Minor. Antiochus was ready to move into the north and west in an attempt to seize that territory and called upon Philip to keep his commitment.

A new cloud was rising on the international scene, however. Rome was a growing power to the west. About 202 BC, Rome had successfully put an end to its conflict with Hannibal. The cessation of this conflict strengthened Rome's position in the Mediterranean world and allowed it to turn its attention eastward to the remnants of Alexander's empire.

Calling for Rome's immediate attention was Philip V of Macedon. First of all, because he had been an ally of Hannibal, he needed to be punished. Second, he was expanding his holdings in accord with his treaties with Antiochus III. If he were successful, he would be a more powerful adversary for Rome. Third, and probably most important, Philip's territory was closer to Rome than that of the Ptolomies or the Seleucids.

War with Rome

In 197 BC, some cities on the Greek peninsula, under attack from Philip V, called upon Rome for help. That was the only excuse Rome needed. Roman troops swept swiftly to the "rescue," decisively defeating Philip and "liberating" the Greek cities. These cities discovered that their "liberation" was much less than what they had wished. They then appealed to Antiochus III for deliverance from their "deliverers." Antiochus did succeed in making a successful landing on the Greek peninsula and did capture some of the cities (193 BC).

Rome, however, was not so easily overcome. In 192 BC, Antiochus III was driven out of Greece and returned to Asia Minor. Rome quickly followed him, crossed the Aegean Sea after defeating him in a major sea battle, and pursued him into Asia. Antiochus sought to stop the Romans quickly and send them home in defeat. However, in a major battle at Magnesia near Ephesus, Antiochus himself was thoroughly defeated (190 BC).

The Peace of Apamea

With no other options open, Antiochus signed a treaty of peace with Rome at Apamea in 188 BC. This treaty had devastating consequences for Antiochus and his successors. Among the terms of the treaty, three stand out for their impact upon our study. First, the son of Antiochus III had to go to Rome as a hostage. He later became Antiochus IV Epiphanes. His experience in Rome influenced his later rule over Palestine with disastrous consequences. Second, Antiochus III and his successors had to give up all claim to any territory west of the Taurus Mountains. This placed a permanent western boundary on the Seleucid empire, forcing more attention on Palestine than it might otherwise have had. The third stipulation of the treaty had the most disastrous consequences. Rome levied a tribute upon Antiochus III in the amount of fifteen thousand talents. This was a tribute so high as to be unknown in the ancient world. To ease it a bit, Rome agreed to allow him to pay it in twelve yearly installments.

For Antiochus III, the payment of the annual tribute became his main concern. Having been stripped of much of his territory, the tax base from which he could have raised these funds was radically lessened. Rather than devoting himself either to the proper administration of his government or to the expansion of his empire, Antiochus was turned into little more than a tax gatherer. It was humiliating to one whose ambitions had been so broad. At the same time, his experience with Rome had been so overwhelming that he did not dare to fail in paying the tribute.

In the ancient world, temples were the site of much wealth. The gifts and payments of the worshipers were stored there. The vessels used in worship were often made of gold and silver. It even appears that temples were used as storehouses or banks for the wealth and possession of the worshipers. Antiochus III, knowing this, determined that temple treasures could serve as the basis from which he could obtain the tribute he needed to pay Rome. Therefore, he set forth to plunder the treasure of the Bel temple in Suisana (Elam). This act so aroused the hostility of the local people that they rioted. He was foolishly unprepared for this reaction and was surprised at the task, overwhelmed, and assassinated. With his death in 187 BC, the reign of Antiochus III (the Great) came to an ignominious end. He who had appeared to be destined for glory died as a thieving tax-collector, a puppet in the hands of Rome.

Seleucus IV Philopator

The successor to the Seleucid throne was Seleucus IV Philopator, the oldest son of Antiochus III. His younger brother, Antiochus, remained a hostage in Rome. He was to be held there until the tribute levied by Rome against the Seleucid kingdom in the Peace of Apamea was paid in full. Under the reign of Seleucus IV, taxes were further increased on the people of Palestine and Syria. Those who had welcomed the transition to being vassals to the Seleucids instead of being Ptolemaic vassals discovered how quickly a situation can change. The taxes which had been reduced during the time of transition became higher than anything ever assessed under the Ptolemies.

During this turbulent and distressing time for Seleucus IV, Ptolemy V (204-181 BC) sought to take advantage of the Seleucid kingdom's distractions. An attempt was planned and apparently initiated to retake Palestine for Egypt. With all the disaffections of the peoples there, it was likely to have been successful. However, the death of Ptolemy V in 181 BC ended the attempt and removed the threat.

Seleucus IV still had the problem of collecting taxes to pay the tribute due to Rome. During this time, he appointed Heliodorus as his prime minister with the major task of collecting revenue from any source possible. It was an all but impossible task. However, as other politicians both before and after Seleucus have discovered, designating impossible tasks to others appears to let you off the hook. If failure comes, as it is expected, someone else can be held responsible.

Heliodorus, as a loyal and grateful (?) appointee, set out to do his master's bidding. He, in addition to all the normal means of collecting taxes, turned to the route of plundering the temples of the Seleucid vassals. At this point, one of the leaders of Jerusalem (we shall return to this later in the chapter) informed Apollonius, the Seleucid governor of the region, that a great deal of treasure, along with the rich vessels and furnishings, was stored in the Temple of Jerusalem. As we shall see, much intrigue among rival factions was going on in Jerusalem at that time. This report (betrayal) was probably an outgrowth of that activity.

When Apollonius's report reached the royal court, Seleucus IV sent Heliodorus to take possession of the treasure. According to 2 Maccabees, Heliodorus was prevented from successfully completing his mission when he was confronted, beaten, and turned away by several supernatural beings. This appears highly unlikely, for in less than twenty years the Temple was not only plundered but desecrated with no supernatural intervention to save it. What does appear certain is that Heliodorus was prevented from plundering the Temple. He may have invented this story, he may have been the victim of a deception, or this may be a later Hebrew invention to explain known facts.

In any case, he returned home without the wealth of the Jerusalem Temple. This certainly would have both displeased and disappointed Seleucus IV. He may have threatened to replace or to punish (by execution?) Heliodorus. In any case, the tables were turned and Seleucus IV was murdered in 175 BC by Heliodorus.

Antiochus IV Epiphanes

Shortly before the death of Seleucus IV, two related events had taken place which were to have far-reaching repercussions at this time. Rome recognized that a brother as a hostage was not of great value. When Seleucus IV had fallen behind in his payment of tribute, Rome insisted that Demetrius, the younger son of Seleucus, be sent to Rome as a hostage to replace his uncle, Antiochus. Upon Antiochus's release, he went to Athens rather than home to Antioch. It was safer; in Antioch he might have been viewed as a rival claimant to the throne of Seleucus.

In Athens, Antiochus won the love and support of the people by his Hellenistic manner of life and his generous giving to temples and other buildings. While in Rome he had become a great admirer of Roman organization and power. His experiences in these two places were to shape his life and future. The opportunity to use these experiences came with the assassination of his brother, Seleucus IV.

Publicly Heliodorus sought only to serve as regent for the older son of Seleucus IV, Antiochus (note that he had the same name as his uncle in Athens), who was still a minor. However, it appears that it was actually Heliodorus's intent to manipulate himself on to the throne. That attempt was quickly thwarted.

Antiochus, in Athens, acted with speed. Legally he was the regent of the Seleucid kingdom. He sought and was granted an army from Eumenes II, the king of Pergamum. There seems to have been little doubt in the mind of either Antiochus or Eumenes II as to what was intended, for the Pergamene king presented Antiochus with numerous kingly gifts, including a crown. The power of Rome was such in this part of the world that it is doubtful if any of this could have happened without her agreement and permission.

Antiochus proceeded rapidly from Athens and quickly put down Heliodorus. At that point, Antiochus assumed the rank of king, not of regent, calling himself Antiochus IV. (The "IV" actually belonged to his nephew, but no one seems to have objected. At least, no one who *survived* objected.) For a period of time, inscriptions on coins indicate that the two Antiochuses were considered to be joint kings. However, troubles in Cilicia during the winter of 170/169 BC took the senior Antiochus away for awhile. During his absence, the younger Antiochus, the legal heir, was murdered by Andronicus. Apparently this was done as a service to the king, but he was absent so that he could not be suspected.

Legally Demetrius, the son of the deceased Seleucus IV, who was a hostage in Rome was now the king. The fact that Rome did not raise this issue reveals how involved it had been all along. For all practical purposes, Antiochus IV was now both supreme and secure upon the Seleucid throne.

For the purposes of this book, three separate strands of the reign of Antiochus IV need to be considered. First among these was his personal life. Here we shall see some quirks of personality which shaped both his character and his rulership. At the very least, a certain amount of instability was characteristic of his public and private life. He was unpredictable. The second strand of the reign of Antiochus IV which must be considered and woven into the whole was his vision of his place and the place of his kingdom in the world of the eastern Mediterranean. He had dreams of restoring the glory of the Seleucid empire. But this vision was clearly tempered by his understanding of the power and authority of Rome. Antiochus IV never perceived himself in any way as a rival of Rome.

The third and most important (at least for our purposes) strand of the life of Antiochus IV involved his relationship with the Jews of Judah and Jerusalem. Here he was either ill-advised or ill-informed or both. His unpredictable personality and his reaction to his failed vision of empire had tragic consequences for Judea. His own folly precipitated the reaction which finally brought his dreams of a renewed empire crashing down upon his head. We shall consider each of these in turn.

Antiochus IV spent years as a hostage in Rome. This gave him a deep and abiding appreciation for Roman power. He may have had many illusions, but had none about the relationship of his kingdom to Rome. He knew that he would never be able to overthrow Rome. Antiochus also had a deep appreciation for the Hellenistic way of life. We have no way of knowing how much of this he carried with him into exile and how much he gained while living in Athens. When he left Athens for the throne of the Seleucids, he was a thoroughgoing apostle for Hellenism. As a part of this, he assumed his partial or actual divinity, applying to himself the Greek title *theos epiphanes,* "god manifest" or "the manifest god." This has been shortened and has come to us in his name, Antiochus Epiphanes. While no problem for most of his empire, this certainly would have been a problem for the Jews in Jerusalem. Further, Antiochus placed the image of Zeus Olympius on the backside of the tetradrachm coin of Antioch. This, too, would have been a problem for his Jewish subjects.

Antiochus Epiphanes was reported to be far more democratic than his despotic predecessors. He wandered the streets of Antioch incognito, played practical jokes upon his companions and friends, and was surprisingly generous. His subjects nicknamed him *epimanes,* meaning "madman." This was an obvious pun on his own self-assumed title of *Epiphanes.*

On the other hand, Antiochus Epiphanes was an able governor and an excellent strategist and organizer of his armies. He had an awareness of the past glory of his kingdom and a vision of what it could be in the future, within the limits imposed by Rome. He accepted the burdens imposed by the Peace of Apamea and sought new and better ways of meeting those obligations, particularly by looking eastward and southward.

He was, apparently, overly sure of himself and his abilities. That was his fatal flaw. In other times he might have been a great man. In the critical issue of dealing with the Jews, he showed that his nickname of *epimanes* may have been accurate. His folly there cost him his kingdom.

Campaigns in Egypt

Politically Antiochus Epiphanes saw Egypt and the Ptolemaic kingdom as the best place to expand his kingdom and as the base from which to draw the wealth with which to pay his debt to Rome. Egypt saw Antiochus's Palestinian territory in much the same light.

In 169 BC, Ptolemy VI raised an army which was intended to recapture Palestine. This, however, played right into the hands of Antiochus Epiphanes, for he was already planning an attack upon Egypt. This development merely accelerated his timing. Being informed of the Ptolemaic plans, Antiochus marched and defeated the Egyptian army before it moved out of the Egyptian desert.

Following this victory, Antiochus invaded Egypt proper, laid siege to and captured Memphis. He pursued those who fled from Memphis and captured the Egyptian king, Ptolemy VI Philometor. The young Egyptian king was, in fact, his nephew. Cleopatra, the mother of Ptolemy VI, was the sister of Antiochus IV.

At that point, Antiochus besieged Alexandria, where the younger brother of Ptolemy VI was claiming the throne for himself. Based on the pleas of several Hellenic ambassadors in Alexandria, Antiochus lifted the siege, restored Ptolemy VI to the throne, left a garrison behind in Pelusium to guarantee the peace, and withdrew.

However, that winter (169/168 BC), Antiochus's two newphews united and attacked the Seleucid garrison. Antiochus was soon back in Egypt. As in the preceding year, the Seleucid armies met no effective resistance from the Egyptian troops.

But Antiochus met resistance from another source. Rome suddenly became aware of what was going on. A special commission was sent by the Roman senate to Antiochus Epiphanes in Egypt. This was its simple message: Evacuate Egypt and leave it alone. Antiochus withdrew reluctantly and with great disappointment and unhappiness. That, too, influenced his relationships with a trouble spot in a region which he clearly controlled, Jerusalem and its environs.

The Oniads and Tobiads

In order to come to understand the third strand of Antiochus IV's activities, we need to back up almost a century to the time of the Third Syrian War (ca. 246-241 BC). This was during the period of Ptolemaic control of Palestine. At that time the high priest in Jerusalem, Onias II, decided to quit paying tribute to the Ptolemies. Although Josephus attributed that decision to the high priest's greed and poor spiritual judgment, it is more likely that it was due to his assumption that the Ptolemies were about to be defeated by Seleucus II. Onias's decision probably indicates some support in Jerusalem for the cause of the Seleucids.

After defeating the Seleucids, Ptolemy III either sent a delegation to Jerusalem, came himself, or more likely did both in an attempt to regain the tribute from Onias II. At this point, Joseph, the son of Tobias stepped forward as the leader of a Jewish group who sought to avoid the military occupation of the Ptolemies. He suggested that the religious power in Jerusalem be separated from the political authority. Ptolemy accepted this with alacrity and appointed Joseph as the political leader. This effectively stripped Onias of most of his power and influence. From this point onward, if not before, these two Jewish leaders and the families which they represented were bitter opponents and the policies and causes which they represented and supported. The two families came to be designated as the Oniads and the Tobiads. It is also possible that supporters of one or the other, whether or not they were related, also carried the same designations. Both families were wealthy, influential, and always eager to undercut the other.

What we know of the Tobiads, even in this early time, indicates that they were probably pro-Hellenistic. They showed little respect for the Jewish Law, but had a great deal of concern for business and economics. They sought to turn Jerusalem into a business and commercial center. The Oniads, on the other hand, had been the high-priestly line at least since 320 BC. They were definitely anti-Hellenistic and were ardent supporters of the Torah. They were not above collaboration with a conquering enemy, as long as it kept them in power.

These two families remained bitter enemies throughout the rest of this era. The Tobiads were apparently more politically astute. They supported the Ptolemies until about 200 BC, when they switched their allegiance to the Seleucids. Because of their willingness to support foreign authority, they generally wielded a great political and economic power in the

Jewish community. The ongoing hostility and conflict between these two families served as the background for the relations which Antiochus the Great had with the Jewish people during the days which we are considering.

As a result of the ongoing conflict between the Oniads and the Tobiads, Onias III, high priest of Jerusalem was in Antioch at the time of the accession of Antiochus Epiphanes to the Seleucid throne. He had been forced to go in order to dispel a series of accusations of disloyalty which had been made against him by the Tobiads in Jerusalem. It appeared that his presence, though fortuitous, was going to secure him the authority in Jerusalem which his family had earlier lost. However, at that time his own brother Jason appeared on the scene. Jason's visit was made with the avowed purpose of helping Onias gain the support from the Seleucid king which he desired.

Jason as High Priest

Unfortunately appearances are not always right. As soon as Jason had an audience with Antiochus IV, he offered the king a major increase in tribute as well as an extra one-time gift if he were to be appointed high priest. This would have appealed to any ruler at any time. At that time, Antiochus was behind in his payments of the heavy tribute which had been levied against his kingdom by the Peace of Apamea. But that was not all.

Jason also requested that Antiochus agree to the creation of a gymnasium in Jerusalem. Finally, the would-be high priest requested that the citizens of Jerusalem be designated Antiochenes. This would have granted the rights of citizenship to them. This was significant because of the Hellenizing tendencies of Antiochus Epiphanes. The offers of Jason were a dream come true for the new king. Jason's offer was accepted, and he was appointed high priest in the place of Onias III.

The appointment of Jason as high priest in Jerusalem was a major new step for the Seleucids. None of the Greek rulers before Antiochus IV had assumed such authority for themselves. In spite of its high-handed nature and the fact that the reigning high priest was still alive, Jason was at least a member of the Zadokite priesthood and had a legitimate claim according to that lineage to serve in the office. Quite likely Jason had the support of the Tobiads in making his approach to Antiochus. The old conflict was still making itself felt. But Jason's high priesthood was quite brief, lasting from about 175 to 172 BC.

Menelaus as High Priest

In 172 BC, Jason sent his annual tribute to Antiochus IV by the hand of Menelaus, a brother of Simon who was the political officer and Temple overseer in Jerusalem. Simon and Menelaus were Tobiads. However, when Menelaus was seen by Antiochus, the emmissary from Jason offered to double the annual tribute if he were appointed high priest. It was no sooner said than done. This was an even greater departure than the appointment of Jason. Jason was a descendent of Zadok. Menelaus was not of that priestly line, if he were a priest at all. No one but descendants of Zadok could serve as high priest. Josephus claimed that Menelaus was no priest at all, but a descendent of the house of Benjamin. That may not have been so, as some scholars argue. Josephus was not always utterly trustworthy. However, that is beside the point. In no case was Menelaus a proper person for that office. By this time, Jews were seeing the office of high priest as something to be bought and sold. And Antiochus was clearly willing to let them pay for it. Jason, recognizing the futility of argument, fled from Jerusalem.

Menelaus's priesthood was not wholly peaceful. He was unable to get together the tribute he had promised Antiochus the Great and was summoned before the king to explain. We do not know what excuse he offered, but it was apparently satisfactory, for he retained the high priesthood. Somewhere about 168 BC Jason revolted and led an army into Jerusalem to try to regain the high priesthood. This revolt may have been triggered by rumors of Antiochus's death. Though successful at first, probably due to surprise, Jason was finally bested and had to flee for his life. He found no refuge until he passed beyond the bounds of the kingdom of the Seleucids and arrived in Sparta.

Antiochus and Jerusalem

Finally, in regard to the political activities of Antiochus Epiphanes against Jerusalem, he is said to have plundered the Temple in Jerusalem. One account dates this in 169 BC, following Antiochus's first campaign in Egypt. The other account dates the plundering in 168 BC, following his great disappointment in Egypt. A thorough study makes it appear that he did it both times. This would have been his way of seeking to obtain the tribute Menelaus had promised. It could also have been an attempted punishment of the city for the revolt of Jason. Finally, it was also likely to have been a way to try to work off his frustration over the defeat in Egypt.

When Antiochus IV came to Jerusalem in 168 BC, he destroyed the walls of the city and built a fortress, the Acra, to dominate the Temple area. Jerusalem was being destroyed as a Temple-city and being turned into a Greek polis with a fortress tower for defense. This was presumably Antiochus's way of preparing to defend Palestine against the Ptolemies. He was forbidden from attacking them, but they were not forbidden from attacking him. This was also Antiochus's first step in the full Hellenization of Jerusalem. Others were quick to follow.

Before proceeding further, we need to note that the Jews viewed the plundering of their Temple in far different terms than did the Seleucid kings. To Antiochus the act was simply one of political, economic, and military necessity. It was not an act of aggression against the Jews' religion. But to the Jews, the acts of the foreign king were events of the highest sacrilege. The fact that he had done this to other temples in his kingdom did not matter. What mattered was that he had moved boldly against the Temple.

At this point 1 Maccabees reports that Antiochus issued a decree aimed at uniting the people in his kingdom: The people were to give up their individual customs. Although such a decree might be believable, no other record even hints at such an order. Not even Josephus suggested that Antiochus IV embarked upon such a policy throughout his kingdom. It does appear that he clearly embarked upon a policy of Hellenizing Jerusalem. The question arises as to why he should have so singled out the Jews at that point (168 BC). No reason of which we know offers any explanation for this act, save one. Granting the ongoing conflict between the Oniads and the Tobiads, the newly won power of the Tobiads with Menelaus's high priesthood, and the Hellenizing tendencies which had long been obvious in the Tobiad line, it would appear that upon Antiochus's visit to Jerusalem the Tobiads suggested that he embark upon a policy of Hellenization. No other suggestion appears to presently fit the facts as we know them so well as this.

As an added impetus to this policy in Jerusalem, Antiochus received a request from the Samaritans asking for four things. They asked to be no longer considered as Jews, that their temple on Gerizim should bear the name of Zeus Hellenios, that they be exempted from taxes, and that they be allowed to continue uninterrupted sabbath observance. Antiochus apparently granted all four requests. The latter surely indicates that there was no widespread religious persecution or attempt at unification. On the other hand, their desire to rename their temple would have surely made the urging of a Hellenizing policy in Jerusalem more logical to the

Seleucid king. If the Samaritans wished to become more Hellenized, what reason did he have to question the urging of the Tobiads that Jerusalem also be Hellenized?

Antiochus, therefore, issued a number of decrees in Jerusalem aimed at the Hellenization of the Jewish religion. Though the Tobiads probably urged the king in this direction, he certainly went beyond their expectations. He ordered that the designation of God in the Temple be changed from "Lord of heaven" to Zeus Olympius. He also ordered a second altar to be set up either in addition to or on top of the existing altar. This is apparently what Daniel called the "abomination of desolations" (Dan. 11:31; 12:11, NASB). Other altars were erected throughout Jerusalem and Judea and sacrifices were ordered to be made upon them. Finally, Antiochus IV ordered that the Jews must sacrifice swine upon these altars. It is possible that Antiochus or some of his advisers might have come up with most of these changes simply as a means of making the worship of the Jews more Hellenistic. The offering of swine flesh, however, almost had to have been thought of by a Jew who knew just how abhorrent this would have been to the orthodox. It appears that this, too, was a suggestion of the Tobiads aimed at offending the orthodox Oniads. Unfortunately, neither Antiochus nor those who advised him realized that there was more involved than simply the feelings or the beliefs of two rival powers in Jerusalem. The common people also felt deeply about their religion. Our records are filled with stories of common people who would rather have died than submit to the new regulations of the king. In some of the villages and towns, the king's altars were pulled down. This was an affront no king could permit, especially one as overbearing as Antiochus. At this point, the stage was set for rebellion. It was not long in coming.

The Hebrews Under the Seleucids

Several major developments occurred within the Hebrew population of Palestine during the days of the Seleucid empire. Some of these were similar to those experienced under the Ptolemies. Part of these were similar, but intensified. Some of these developments were decidedly new.

Political Developments

From a political and military standpoint, the first and perhaps most important development was the end of the Fifth Syrian War (201-198 BC) which brought an end as well to the century-old struggle between the Seleucids and the Ptolemies over the possession and control of Palestine. The victory won by Antiochus III (the Great) brought the territory of the Jews, as well as all Palestine, under the control of the Seleucids.

This transition was immediately hailed as a great deliverance by at least two groups of Jews. First, those among the leaders of the Hebrews who were anti-Egyptian or pro-Seleucid were pleased. These were mainly Oniads. Their reason was simple: Their side had won. Because of their prior support of the Seleucids or, more openly, their opposition to the Egyptians, they expected to reap the political rewards of power and patronage. Unfortunately, in this they were thwarted, for they were also dealing among their own people with some of the more astute politicians who ever lived, the Tobiads. The Tobiads had the political acumen to switch sides just before the Seleucid victory. For a number of reasons which we shall examine later, the Tobiads were able to capitalize upon their new position better than the Oniads were able to use their older platform.

The second group pleased by the transition to Seleucid control were the people who felt the bite of the tax collector. This included the priests, the merchants and traders, and the wealthy. One of the first acts of Antiochus III, after gaining control of Palestine, was the reduction of taxes. This is always an act to win the favor of people.

The change of empires brought a decided sense of relief among the powerful people of Jerusalem. To Antiochus III these were the people who mattered. Insofar as the Jews were concerned, those were also the ones who mattered. Both major political parties, most (if not all) of the people of prominence and power, and persons of means welcomed the coming of the new ruler. Those citizens who still supported Egyptian suzerainty kept relatively quiet about it for the time being.

From the standpoint of the common people, the transition from Ptolemaic to Seleucid control brought little noticeable change. Taxes may have been less, but to these people, taxes were always a burden. Politically, the rule of one foreign ruler was not appreciably different from that of another. The only real change which they may have noticed was the absence of the ongoing series of wars. At the very least, foreign troops would not have been marching through their land so frequently. At the most, they would have been delivered from the steady threat of being forced or invited to join an army on its way to war. For a time, the coming of the Seleucids seemed to bring peace and rest to the land. That was welcomed by all.

In a brief digression, we need to consider why the Tobiad switch of support to the Seleucids may have ultimately been more influential than the Oniad longer-term support. The Oniads were priests, descendants of the line of Zadok. Their major concern was with the faith of Israel and the outward manifestation of that faith: sacrifice, ritual purity, sabbath observance, circumcision, and the basic requirements of the Holiness Code; in short, orthodoxy. Collaboration with foreign rulers was acceptable only so far and no farther.

The Tobiads, on the other hand, operated with a different code of ethics. They were not as concerned with ethics as they were with power and prosperity. They were genuine Hellenists, seeking to make or to remake their society into a copy of the Greek culture which had so swept the world. There was almost nothing they would not do or agree to in order to gain power and wealth. This was justified on the basis that it would bring peace and stability to their land within the empire. Because they were willing to go much farther in their collaboration, they were able to win more support from Antiochus III. It was that simple. Their own life-style allowed them to offer more to the Seleucid rulers. For that reason, even though they were late in their support, they were received more readily and rewarded with more largess.

Parties Within Judaism

We have noted at least twice before in this chapter the on-going conflict between the two major parties or families within Jerusalem, the Oniads and the Tobiads. The Oniads were priestly and orthodox. They were willing to collaborate with their rulers in order to maintain their authority. However, they were highly orthodox and would not collaborate when it meant a major compromise with their faith. During the preceding century, all the high priests came from their family.

Both in conflict and in contrast to the Oniads was the family of Tobiads. They were people of wealth and probably nonpriestly in lineage. One source describes them as Benjamites, descendants of the tribe of Benjamin. Some scholars argue that by the process of intermarriage across tribal lines, there was a legitimate claim to a priestly heritage. That may be so, although I remain unconvinced. However, even if a priestly heritage were present among the Tobiads, they were not descended from Zadok and had no legitimate claim to the high priesthood. The Tobiads were boldly Hellenistic. They also appear almost to have been evangelists for Hellenism. They, by their collaboration, had gathered to themselves both political power and the authority to collect taxes during the last part of the Ptolemaic period. This brought great wealth to their family and party. They appear to have considered their traditional faith outdated and were willing to collaborate to almost any length in order to maintain or to increase their wealth, power, and influence. A major factor of this period of Seleucid control over Jerusalem was the open conflict between the Oniads and the Tobiads.

A third party of the Jews is quite significant near the end of this era, the Hasidim (or Hasidaeans, as 1 and 2 Maccabees identifies them). Unlike the other two parties, the Hasidim were not related to a particular family. Neither were they limited to the wealthy and powerful. At the beginning, the Hasidim were primarily made up of common people and were led by rabbis and priests of lesser significance than the Zadokites. The name of the party literally describes them, for these were "the pious ones." Their primary concern was to hold on to the faith of their fathers with no compromise or collaboration. We do not know exactly when this group began. It must have been during a time when Hellenizing and collaboration were being pushed by the leaders of Jerusalem. The Hasidim could have had their roots in the time of Ptolemaic control. However, the Seleucid era offered a fertile time for their growth, if not their birth.

From the earliest references, it is clear that both the Oniads and the Tobiads despised the Hasidim. This may have been because the concerns of the Hasidim struck a tender nerve and aroused a guilty conscience on the part of the two parties of power. These considered the Hasidim to be hopelessly outdated in their concerns and attitudes. However, in the long term, the Hasidim offered real leadership to the Jews and gave Judaism its ultimate shape. The Hasidim also were in part the ancestors of the Pharisees.

The Crisis of the Priesthood

From about 320 BC, the high priests in Jerusalem had been Oniads. Descended from Onias I, they were all Zadokite priests, descendants of Zadok, a priest of David and a supporter of Solomon in the conflict over David's successor (1 Kings 1:38-39). From the time of Solomon, Zadokite priests were considered to be the genuine line of high priests. In the post-Exilic period and particularly in the time following the victories of Alexander the Great, the high priest of Jerusalem became both the political and the cultic ruler of Jerusalem. He was subject generally only to the territorial governor and then to the reigning king himself. This gave the Oniads great power.

In the time of the reign of Ptolemy IV Philopator of Egypt, all that changed. At that time, Onias II, high priest of Jerusalem, expected Egypt to lose the Fourth Syrian War (221-217 BC). In consequence of his belief, he withheld the payment of the annual tribute to Ptolemy IV. When the war was over, Ptolemy was the victor. The collection of taxes is the chief business of conquerors. Therefore, Ptolemy immediately took steps to collect his back taxes. It was then that Joseph of the house of Tobias stepped forward, bought the right to collect taxes, and was given the position of chief political officer in Jerusalem and Judea. Thus the high priest was stripped of all secular authority. At the same time, the disagreements and the conflict between the Oniads and the Tobiads was accelerated and moved into the open. In a real sense, this was the first step in Jerusalem's crisis of the priesthood. This occurred well before the period of Seleucid rule. This policy, however, was confirmed and continued when Antiochus III overthrew the Ptolemaic control of Palestine in 198 BC at the conclusion of the Fifth Syrian War (201-198 BC).

Things did not change much during the next few years. However, everything was altered when Antiochus IV Epiphanes ascended to the throne in 175 BC. Just before his accession to the throne, Simon, captain of the Temple and a Tobiad, had made numerous and continuous charges against Onias III who was high priest. Onias III had gone (or had been summoned) to Antioch to deal with those charges. He was in the capital when Seleucus IV died and when Antiochus Epiphanes became king. Onias sought in those early days of Antiochus IV to consolidate his position as high priest. All appeared to be going well when Jason, the brother of Onias III, showed up to offer aid. When Jason was given an audience with Antiochus Epiphanes, however, he offered to double the annual tribute and to make a one-time extra payment to the king. The offer was immediately accepted and Jason was appointed high priest in 175 BC.

This high-handed act of Antiochus was possibly legal from a Jewish standpoint, but it was a major departure from precedent. The reigning high priest was still alive, and no charges had been brought against him, much less been proven, sufficient to warrant removal from the priesthood. Appointing a successor at such a time was unheard of. Nonetheless, it was done. This was the second step in the developing crisis of the priesthood. It was almost certainly supported by the Tobiads.

The third step in the developing crisis of the priesthood occurred only three years later, in 172 BC. When Jason became high priest, among his closest associates was a man named Menelaus, the son of Simon the Tobiad who had given Onias III so much trouble. This relationship makes us conclude that Jason was supported by the Tobiads. In 172 BC,

Jason sent Menelaus to Antioch with the annual payment of tribute. But Menelaus carried more than Jerusalem's taxes.

When Menelaus was given an audience with the Antiochus Epiphanes, he offered to double again the annual tribute if he were made high priest. To Antiochus, this was nothing but good business. He had sold the priesthood once, why not do it again? To the Jews, it was a horrible development. Menelaus does not even appear to have been a priest. At the very best, he had no claim to be high priest. Yet, by the royal edict of a pagan king, Menelaus the Tobiad was the new high priest in Jerusalem. The crisis of the priesthood was at hand.

The Crisis of the Cult

Many things could be said to be a part of the crisis of the cult at Jerusalem. However, the major ones with which we are concerned arose under the reign of Antiochus IV Epiphanes following his aborted Egyptian campaign in 168 BC.

By cult, I refer to the worship of the Jews in Jerusalem. The term covers their ritual, the worship personnel, the objects and trappings of worship, and their outward religious symbols.

Following Menealus's appointment as high priest, Jason fled to the Transjordan region. However, during the second Egyptian campaign of Antiochus Epiphanes, rumors reached Jerusalem not only that he had been defeated but that he was dead. This news, false though it was, served as the basis for an attempt by Jason to regain the high priesthood. He made a swift raid on Jerusalem and briefly drove Menelaus from the Temple. Even though Jason at first had been suspect, to the Hasidim he was certainly an improvement over an illegitimate Tobiad claimant.

Jason's success was short-lived, however. Antiochus Epiphanes, hale and hearty, approached Jerusalem. He was angered over his confrontation with Rome in Egypt. His anger was intensified by the rebellion in Jerusalem. His presence in Jerusalem forced Jason to flee, and Menelaus was reinstated in the high priesthood.

The Tobiads apparently convinced Antiochus IV that the only way to bring Jerusalem into line with the king's goals and plans was to Hellenize it thoroughly. This advice shows just how far out of touch they were with the real feelings of the people and with the power and influence of the Hasidim.

Antiochus Epiphanes embarked upon a policy of major and deliberate confrontation. An altar to Zeus was erected on top of or in place of the altar to Yahweh, the Lord of heaven. Other altars to Zeus were erected throughout Jerusalem and the land. Circumcision and sabbath observance were forbidden. Swine flesh was to be sacrificed and eaten by all Jews. And the penalty for disobedience of these policies was death.

In one fell swoop, all that the faithful in Jerusalem and Judea loved and prized was taken away. Other policies of Antiochus had struck primarily at the wealthy and powerful, leaving the people basically alone. This policy produced a cultic crisis which was felt by every faithful Jew in the land. This crisis of the Jerusalem cult was the last and biggest mistake of Antiochus Epiphanes. Its repercussions were to strip Jerusalem and Judea from his control and to change the course of history. The ill-advised and ill-implemented Hellenizing policy of Antiochus Epiphanes showed not only how out of touch the Tobiads were with the situation in Jerusalem but also how poor was the choice of advisers which Antiochus had made. He apparently never understood why the Jewish people reacted so violently to his policy. His advisers should have, and could have, warned him of the possible consequence of his edicts.

The Reaction of the People

Peace, warmth, and friendship win the support of people, even conquered people. But striking with power at the things they hold most dear arouses deep feelings and creates stiff resistance. The Jewish people, the ordinary folk who made up the backbone and heart and sinew of the nation, were appalled at the abhorrent policies of Antiochus Epiphanes. With the leadership and encouragement of the Hasidim, the people decided to resist. This was no decision made from the top. The people who had never been involved in politics before made this decision. By ones and twos, then by tens and twenties, they decided that faith was more important than life. The people believed Antiochus IV would carry out his dreaded policy. They feared the king, and rightly so. But they feared God more. The ordinary common folk simply, quietly, and calmly decided to resist. Theirs was no organized revolt. Neither was it a militant resistance. They simply decided with cold logic to remain faithful to God, regardless of the cost. Few experiences in history stand out like this one for heroism, commitment, devotion, and calm but agonizing suffering.

In Jerusalem, mothers continued to have their baby boys circumcised. Antiochus IV's soldiers killed the infants, tied their bodies around their mother's necks and forced the women to parade through the streets. Finally the women were executed. Yet, having witnessed this, other mothers then circumcised their sons.

An aged scribe was forced to eat pork, but spit it out, refusing to swallow it. He was offered another chance, and some of his friends urged him to bring clean and proper meat and substitute it for the swine flesh and pretend to eat it. He worried about the effect such an act might have on younger people and refused. As a consequence, he was beaten to death.

An aged woman and her seven grown sons were brought forward to be forced to eat pork. When they refused, each in turn had his tongue cut out, his hands cut off, and then was literally cooked alive. Finally the mother herself was executed in a similar manner. The worse the persecution became, the more people joined the faithful.

Many people went out into the caves in the hill country to observe the sabbath. Antiochus sent his soldiers after them. When the soldiers discovered that the Jews would not defend themselves on the sabbath, they chose that time to attack. In these attacks, they barricaded the people inside the caves and burned them alive.

The resistance spread. So did the persecution. Each fed upon the other. Finally, the soldiers of Antiochus Epiphanes spread through the countryside, seeking to put down what to them was a rebellion. But it was like no rebellion they had ever encountered. It was passive, not active. It was submissive, not offensive. The oppression increased. The will to resist became more certain, included more people, spread to more centers. An explosion was coming.

5
The Maccabean Revolt
(167-142 BC)

The radical Hellenizing policy of Antiochus IV Epiphanes had set the stage for rebellion. His desecration of the Temple in Jerusalem had occurred in December 168 BC. That marked the beginning of the pressure to turn Jerusalem and Judea into a Hellenistic center. Antiochus's edicts and the enforcement of them drove the Hasidim, the pious ones, to desperation.

A theological development apparently determined the earliest form which the Jewish resistance toward Antiochus's policies took. Throughout most of the Old Testament era, there had been little hope for resurrection or of life after death. Occasional glimpses of such a hope may be seen, but most of the people in Old Testament times found their hope for the future simply in living on through their children. This concept made having male children to carry on the family line important. However, during the interbiblical period, a growing number of Jewish people accepted the concept of life after death. This established the foundation for the full-blown belief in an afterlife which the New Testament teaches.

The significance of this belief for the days leading up to and including the beginning of the Maccabean Revolt cannot be minimized. When people believe that life with God goes on after death, death loses much of its terror for it loses much of its sense of finality. This new dimension of the Jewish faith offers a partial explanation for the willingness of many Jews to resist passively and die rather than participate in the pagan cult which Antiochus Epiphanes sought to establish in Jerusalem. However, passive resistance soon gave way to other measures of resistance.

Chronological Table
The Maccabean Revolt (167-142 BC)

Egypt	Syria	Judea	High Priests
Ptolemy VI	Antiochus IV	Judas	Menelaus

(181-145)	Epiphanes (175-164)	(167-161)	(172-162)
		Dedication of the Temple (165)	
	Antiochus V Enpator (164-162)	Syrian Peace Treaty (163/162)	
		Roman Treaty (162/161)	
	Demetrius I (162-150)		Alcimus (162-159)
		Jonathan (161-142)	Intersacerdo- tum (159- 152)
	Alexander Balas (150-145)		
			Jonathan (152-142)
Ptolemy VII (145)	Demetrius II (145-138)		
Ptolemy VIII (145-116)	Antiochus VI (145-142)		
	Trypho (142-138)		

The Revolt Itself (167-161 BC)

Mattathias's Act

Events came to a head in the village of Modein in 167 BC. The delegation from Antiochus Epiphanes sought to force Mattathias, a priest, and an elder of the village, to sacrifice swine flesh to Zeus. The old priest was promised a gift from the king for so doing. With utter disdain for the royal embassy, Mattathias boldly asserted his loyalty to the faith of his fathers regardless of the practice and policy of others or of the threats and punishment of the king. Neither fear nor greed would move him to apostatize. When another village leader stepped forward to do the royal bidding, Mattathias was overcome with fury. In a violent outburst, he slew the traitor upon the altar, killed the royal commissioner, and then pulled the altar down. After that he boldly issued a call to followers of the Torah and the covenant to follow him into the wilderness.

With the act of Mattathias, the die was cast. No king could ignore such a direct repudiation of royal policy. Certainly Antiochus Epiphanes would not. Even more directly, no king could allow the assassination of a royal messenger to go unpunished. Antiochus did not.

Mattathias had no false illusions about the consequences of his act. The revolt, once started, was pushed to its limits. Mattathias led his five sons, Judas, John, Simon, Jonathan, and Eleazar, into the wilderness of the central hill country where they established themselves in caves. Many supporters came from the villages round about. Perhaps a significant observation is that this rebellion in its initial stages was supported by the rural and village areas. Most of our study to this point has focused upon the cities, especially Jerusalem. Whatever else may be said of it, this revolt was of the common people.

Besides this, two other significant features of the rebellion should be noted. First, the Hasidim immediately lent their support. These "pious ones" saw in the act and cause of Mattathias their best hope for overthrowing the pagan Hellenistic forces which threatened their faith and way of life. Their support made it even more of a populist or popular movement. The second major additional feature of the revolt was that, initially, it took the shape of Jew against Jew, rather than of Jew against pagan. The initial attacks by Mattathias and his followers were directed against Hellenized Jews. Hurried, hit-and-run, guerrilla-type raids were carried out under cover of darkness. Homes and villages of collaborators and apostates were destroyed and put to the torch.

Before long the local forces of the Seleucid empire began to react. When it was seen that the Hasidim refused to fight on the sabbath, major attacks by the forces of Antiochus IV delayed their attacks until then. The results were the slaughter of orthodox Jewish supporters of the revolt. At that time Mattathias and his sons decided they had to defend themselves whenever they were attacked, even on the sabbath. This decision created problems for some of the Hasidim and marked the beginning of a break in their relationship to and support of the revolt. On the other hand, others of the Hasidim, less idealistic and more practical, became more involved with the revolt.

These early days were days of stress, organization, and constant activity. They took their toll upon the health of the aged Mattathias. It was not long until he died (ca. 167/166 BC).

Judas the Maccabee and His Early Victories

Upon the death of Mattathias, his son Judas assumed command of the rebel forces. We have no explanation for this development since leadership would have been expected to descend to the eldest son. Judas became known as "Maccabee." This nickname was assigned only to him and either meant "the Piercer" or "the Hammer." The latter explanation is accepted by the majority of scholars. So significant was his leadership that his nickname was given to the entire movement, and it has come to be known as the Maccabean Revolt. His family is called the Maccabees by many. Lest we become confused, Mattathias was descended from the family of Hashmon, and the family is also called the Hasmoneans from that name.

For a time, Judas continued his guerrilla-type attacks. The rebel forces had grown to about six thousand soldiers. In 166 BC, they had their first confrontation with sizable Seleucid armies. The first of these was led by Apollonius, the governor of Judea and Samaria, and the second was led by the Seleucid general Seron. In both battles, Judas was victorious. Apollonius was killed in battle. The site of the first battle is unknown, but the second was fought at Beth-horon.

The significance of these victories cannot be overestimated. Certainly the Jewish troops were fighting over terrain with which they were intimately familiar. They were also motivated by religious zeal. But they were essentially untrained troops facing an experienced, organized army which was accustomed to victory. This was the first time a Jewish army had truly taken to the field since Babylon overthrew Judah more than four centuries earlier.

Initially the Syrian leaders wholly underestimated the significance of the revolt. But these early successes on the part of Judas got their attention. At the first Antiochus IV had been concerned with a Parthian campaign in the east. That continued to be the center of his attention. But before he departed for those regions about 166 BC, he ordered his prime minister, Lysias, to stamp out the Jewish revolt. Lysias, in turn, sent three armies to Judea. They were met and defeated by Judas and

his troops near Emmaus. Later the same year, Lysias led an army southward. A major battle was fought near Beth-zur. While it is doubtful if
this could be called a total victory for Judas, the Syrian army did retreat
to Antioch. Syria had conducted three major campaigns against Judas,
and Judas had won all three. Syria entered into some form of peace
negotiations with Judas at that time. With the drain which Antiochus's
campaigns were making on resources, something had to be done to bring
relief. Also, Rome apparently got involved in the negotiations. It was to
Rome's best interest to aggravate and irritate nations on the edge of the
empire without having to intervene directly with troops. They apparently
were putting pressure on Syria to leave Judea alone. The sources are
neither clear nor utterly dependable at this point. We cannot say with
certainty that a formal peace treaty was concluded. But at least Judas
felt more freedom than at any prior time. At least, he had a truce with
Syria. We need to remember that the rebellion was rooted in religious
concerns. The continual emphasis upon these show that they were a
major part of the campaign. This brief respite from outside military
intervention gave Judas the opportunity to fulfill one of his basic purposes, the reversal of the apostasy of Hellenism.

The Temple Rededication

Judas's three victories over the Syrian armies in 166 BC and early 165
BC left Syria's military resources in the region of Palestine depleted.
When he became aware that Antiochus and his armies were off in the
east and that they were not immediately going to attack again, Judas
decided to take advantage of the situation. He made plans to retake the
Temple. Part of his troops were assigned the task of keeping the Syrian
garrison in the Acra at bay. Under the leadership of the Jewish priests,
the Temple was thoroughly cleansed. Menelaus, the high priest, is not
mentioned. He had collaborated with (and possibly instigated) Antiochus Epiphanes's Hellenization of the land and the Temple precincts.
Thus, he was apparently wholly ignored by Judas and his Maccabean
supporters.

The altar to Zeus was destroyed and removed from the Temple and
a new altar was built. The furnishings and vessels were repaired or made
new as needed and as the law permitted. The Temple and its precincts
were repaired and cleansed. Finally a great festival of dedication was
scheduled. Beginning on the twenty-fifth of Chislev (essentially compar-
able to our December) in 165 BC, the Temple was rededicated. The
festival of exuberant joy lasted eight days, and the Jewish leaders decreed

that it be held annually. It was added to the Jewish religious calendar as Hanukkah ("dedication"). The festival became popularly known as the Feast of Lights.

Josephus, seeking to emphasize the sovereign providence of God, stated that the rededication occurred exactly three years to the day from the time of its desecration. However, sources indicate that orthodox Jewish sacrifice in the Temple stopped in mid year. There is little question but that Josephus created his facts to match his theology. The period of the Temple's disuse was probably more in the neighborhood of two-and-a-half years.

No opposition to the cleansing and rededication of the Temple was apparently offered by the Syrian garrison in the Acra. The presence of Judas's army there is not sufficient to explain this by itself. Almost certainly, the negotiations between Judas and Lysias in the early part of the year had resulted in that garrison's being ordered, at the very least, to be nonaggressive in its relationship with the Maccabean forces. Judas apparently even fortified the Temple precincts at that time with no opposition from the Syrians. However, these conditions were not to last long.

Other Conflicts

For the next three or four years, in order to understand the events centering upon the revolt, we will need to follow several different developments throughout the empire. The details are not all clear, but I shall seek to keep them as uncomplicated as possible.

With the dedication of the Temple, the original goal of the revolt, religious freedom, had been attained. However, in early 164 BC, communities of orthodox Jews in Galilee and Gilead appealed to Judas to rescue them from the oppressions of their Hellenistic neighbors. Judas and Jonathan led an expedition to Galilee, and Simon led one to Gilead. Both were successful, bringing the Jews from those regions back into Jerusalem.

These victories, coupled with his earlier successes emboldened Judas to the point of folly. He became convinced of the absolute support of God, the invincibility of his troops, and the utter correctness of his own strategy. He was wrong on all points. Although there is some disagreement on the interpretation of the facts, Judas began a series of attacks upon territory surrounding Judea, apparently seeking to gain land and build a kingdom, if not an empire. He undertook campaigns to the east in Transjordan, to the south in Idumea (formerly Edom), and to the west in the Philistine plain that were successful. Obviously, these campaigns all took time. Just as obviously, these victorious expansionistic advances were a far more serious threat to Syria than anything which he had done before. Messages of his victories clearly had to have reached Antioch. Yet for an entire year the Seleucid empire allowed him to proceed unchecked, even unthreatened. Why? We must turn to the center of the empire for an answer to that puzzle.

A hurried survey offers at least some solution to our problem. When Antiochus IV Epiphanes had departed from Antioch on his Parthian campaign, he had left his minor son, Antiochus Eupator in the care of Lysias. Further, he had appointed Lysias as regent of the kingdom in his absence. The campaign in the east had been quite successful, but it had drained the resources of the empire. Frankly, in 164 BC, Lysias simply did not have adequate troops or supplies to make a major campaign into Judea. And a major campaign was obviously needed. No mere half-hearted measures were going to be sufficient. Even more important, in 164 BC, Antiochus IV died in Parthia. On his deathbed, however, he appointed Philip, a general who was with him, as guardian of his son, the boy-king Eupator. This was an unexplained threat to Lysias that stripped him of at least half of his power. However, Antiochus Eupator was in Antioch with Lysias, and Lysias was not about to give up the boy-king without a fight. He spent the better part of that year consolidating his hold upon the central part of the empire and making sure that all of the reins of government were firmly in his grasp. Ignoring the wishes of his dead ruler, he continued to be both regent and guardian. He knew that shortly he would have to face Philip who had been appointed guardian. He wished to be as prepared as possible when that time came.

At this point, probably in early 163 BC, Judas laid siege to the Acra and its occupants. To the orthodox Jews, and particularly to the Hasidim, a foreign garrison overlooking the Temple was no longer acceptable. It is one thing to win battles in the field. It is quite another to seize a well-built, well-supplied, and well-defended fortress. Judas and his troops were in a different situation than they had faced before. Meanwhile, messengers fled from the Acra to Lysias, appealing for help.

Lysias marched southward, taking the boy-king Eupator with him. Seeking to outflank Judas, Lysias attacked Judea from the south. He first attacked and destroyed Beth-zur. Moving northward, he fought a major battle near Beth-zacharias. This was the first time that the Maccabees had faced an army using elephants. It was obviously a terrifying experience, giving the Syrians an advantage which was hard to overcome.

Judas's brother Eleazar saw one elephant particularly decked out with ornaments and armor and assumed that the king was upon him. He raced under the elephant, thrust his spear into its heart and killed it. Unfortunately, when the elephant died, it fell upon Eleazar crushing him. Eleazar's sacrifice had all been for nothing, for no person of significance was upon the elephant. Judas, realizing that he could not face such an army, withdrew to the Temple fortress.

The army of Lysias proceeded to Jerusalem and laid siege to the sanctuary. It appeared that all was about to be lost. Such was not the case. At that moment, Lysias heard that Philip had arrived in Antioch with an army and was asserting his claims to the guardianship and to the regency. Lysias was in a desperate situation. He needed to be in Antioch, and he could not leave Jerusalem. Judas made the most of the situation. A peace was agreed upon that restored all the religious freedom the Jews had enjoyed before the Hellenization of Antiochus Epiphanes was begun. Further, a full pardon and amnesty was granted to all the rebels. Menelaus was executed, removing that thorn from the side of the Hasidim. On the other hand, Judas was forced to destroy his fortification of the Temple and the garrison at the Acra was allowed to remain for the sake of maintaining the peace. A new Syrian governor was appointed. Upon this, Lysias raced for Antioch.

Religious freedom, which had been won in 165 BC, was now made firm by a treaty in late 163 or 162 BC. Yet Judas was not satisfied. His goals were now clearly political freedom as well.

Back in Rome, however, other developments had been taking place. Upon Antiochus Epiphanes's death in 164 BC, his young son had inherited the throne of the Syrian empire. But Demetrius, the son of Seleucus IV and nephew to Antiochus IV, sought to become king. He escaped from Rome and arrived in Antioch about 162 BC. Fearing the conflict between Lysias and Philip and the inadequacies of a boy-king, the people welcomed Demetrius as a conquering hero. He had Antiochus V Eupator executed and was crowned king as Demetrius I. Demetrius was a fugitive from Rome, however, and that did not bode well for his future.

In late 162 or early 161 BC, Judas sought to take advantage of this by entering into a treaty with Rome. Rome was still trying to create problems in the eastern Mediterranean, but lacked the power to enforce all their real interests there. Rome immediately informed Demetrius I that it recognized the political independency of Judea.

However, another event had taken place which made Demetrius ignore Rome's warning. Having left there so recently, he was probably more aware than most of the fact that Rome could not at that point easily enforce any concerns in that part of the world.

Demetrius had appointed Alcimus a successor to Menelaus as high priest in Jerusalem. Alcimus was a descendant of Aaron and thus a legitimate priest. However, he was apparently not a Zadokite. Apparently expecting trouble, Demetrius sent Alcimus to Jerusalem with an army led by Bacchides. As a priest of Aaron, Alcimus was welcomed by the Hasidim. Each pledged friendship and support to the other. However, in a high-handed demonstration of power, Alcimus soon had some sixty Hasidim slaughtered as punishment for prior acts.

Judas and his followers had never accepted Alcimus, leading some interpreters to suppose that they desired the high priesthood for themselves. The brutality of Alcimus swept away much of his initial support. Bacchides, meanwhile, believed that Alcimus had everything under control and returned to Antioch. Judas and his forces drove Alcimus from the Temple and refused to allow him to function.

Bacchides, now governor, sent Nicanor back to Jerusalem to install and maintain Alcimus as high priest. Nicanor entered into a treaty with Judas which displeased Alcimus. He complained again to Demetrius, who ordered Nicanor to capture Judas alive. A major battle was fought near Samaria in the region of Beth-horon, where the Syrians were defeated and Nicanor was killed. Bacchides himself was soon in the land. This army was so overwhelming that the army of Judas simply lost heart and fled. He was left with about eight hundred men. Bravely, but foolishly, Judas stood and faced the enemy. At a place identified as Elasa whose location is now unknown, the mismatched armies met. Following a brave but futile struggle, the Jews were overwhelmed, and Judas was killed (161 BC). He was a courageous general and a brilliant leader. He was also human and had human weaknesses. Yet when he died, it was legitimately said of him, "How is the mighty fallen, the savior of Israel!" (1 Macc. 9:21, RSV).

The Following Years (161-142 BC)

The Seleucid Developments

As is so frequently the case in history, events in locations far removed from the place under study make major impacts on the situation there. Once again, events in the capital of the Seleucid kingdom affected events in Jerusalem and Judea. Throughout this entire era, the situation in

Antioch can be described as chaotic, simply one power struggle after another.

Demetrius I ruled very tenuously for about a decade. Then, about 152 BC, a young man named Balas landed at Ptolemais on the northern coast of Palestine. He identified himself as Alexander Epiphanes, the younger son of Antiochus IV Epiphanes. If this claim were true, he had a legitimate title to the throne of the Seleucids. Demetrius claimed that he was only an adventurer from Ephesus, pretending to have a claim on the throne. On the other hand, Ptolemy VI of Egypt, who had every reason to create problems for the Seleucids, recognized Alexander Balas as Syria's legitimate king and promised to seal that commitment by giving him one of the Egyptian's daughters in marriage. Furthermore, Rome, who also did not have an unbiased attitude, supported the claims of Balas with a senatorial edict.

With civil war in the offing, both Balas and Demetrius needed all the help they could get. Both made large offers to Jonathan (the successor of Judas) and the Jews. The two rivals met in battle in 150 BC, Demetrius was killed, and Alexander Balas became king. He was ruling, however, as an immediate vassal to Egypt and an ultimate vassal of Rome. Ptolemy VI fulfilled his promise and Alexander Balas married Cleopatra Thea.

When Demetrius I died, he left two sons. The younger of these, also named Demetrius, invaded Phoenicia with the support of an army of mercenaries led by Lasthenes. Ptolemy VI, eager to weaken further the Seleucids, marched from Egypt as though to aid Alexander Balas. However, as he marched he seized the cities along the coast of Palestine. When he crossed into Syria, as F. F. Bruce so ably puts it, "he transferred his support—and his daughter—from Balas to Demetrius" (p. 164). The terms for this were that Palestine be returned to Ptolemaic control. Demetrius had no option but to accede to these demands. But when Ptolemy and Demetrius met Alexander Balas in battle in 145 BC, Demetrius came out lucky. Both Alexander Balas and Ptolemy VI were killed. In one confrontation he became Demetrius II, king of Syria and at the same time avoided yielding control of Palestine.

Demetrius II, however, threw his new-won power away by two concurrent mistakes. He severely punished the supporters of Alexander Balas in Antioch and at the same time dismissed his army of mercenaries. The cruel punishment brought a rebellion in Antioch, and the mercenary army was looking for a new cause.

Before Alexander Balas's death, he had left his infant son under the guardianship of an Arabian chieftain. However, an officer from Balas's defeated army by the name of Trypho saw an opportunity to take advantage of this and the two mistakes of Demetrius II.

Trypho had the son transferred to his care and proclaimed him to be king Antiochus VI Epiphanes Dionysus of Syria. Mercenary soldiers are just that, they fight for money and not for a cause. Trypho employed them and was also able to employ the elephant-troops of the deceased Ptolemy VI. He then invaded the central regions of the empire in another civil war for the Seleucid empire. Technically, Syria now had two kings, Demetrius II and the infant Antiochus VI, whose authority was exercised by the regent Trypho. But Trypho was not long content with this. When he felt secure enough, he had Antiochus VI assassinated (ca. 142 BC) and was himself proclaimed king. The political situation in Syria was actually unchanged. They still had two kings, but now they were Demetrius II and Trypho.

Jonathan (161-142 BC)

Following the death of Judas, three of Mattathias' sons still survived, John, Jonathan, and Simon. Eleazar had been crushed by an elephant. The Maccabean forces had essentially disintegrated. The remnants were back among the caves of the central hill country. Technically, since only Judas was called Maccabee, these forces should no longer be called Maccabean. However, since his influence was still strong, I shall call them by that title throughout this chapter, reverting to Hasmoneans (after the family ancestor, Hashmon) in the following chapters.

In the immediate period after Judas's death, Bacchides remained in the land, consolidating his control with strategic fortifications and the seizing of hostages. During this period, John was assassinated by some Nabateans. Also about this time, or shortly thereafter, Alcimus died. He suffered a stroke while supervising the removal of the wall of Judas. The Maccabees saw this as divine judgment. Some date his death a bit earlier and others as late as 153 BC. However, the date 160/159 BC appears more accurate. Following Alcimus's death, Jerusalem went for seven years without a high priest until about 152 BC. We do not know why this gap was allowed. The confused affairs both in Jerusalem and Antioch clearly played their part, but no satisfactory reason to explain this has yet been suggested.

Leadership of the Jewish forces then fell upon Jonathan. Not as able a general nor as charismatic a leader, Jonathan was apparently far more able as a politician and diplomat. About 159 BC, Bacchides felt affairs were secure in Jerusalem and Judea and returned to Antioch. Within two years, however, Jonathan began to seek to strengthen his positions in Judea. This alarmed the Hellenists, who sent for help again.

In 157 BC, Bacchides was back in Judea. He fought with Jonathan at Beth-basi, east of Bethlehem. Bacchides was defeated and entered into a treaty of peace with Jonathan. Jonathan established himself at Michmash and for the next five years lived almost as David had during the reign of Saul. A general time of peace ensued, and Jonathan was able to use this time to consolidate his forces and his authority.

At this time, Alexander Balas appeared on the scene (152 BC). The rivalry between him and Demetrius I gave Jonathan the opportunity he needed. He was politically astute enough to exploit it to the fullest. Demetrius I offered very generous terms of peace and power to Jonathan in return for his support. Balas, on the other hand, with more to gain and nothing to lose, offered even greater concessions, establishing Jonathan as a "Friend and Ally of the King." More significantly, Alexander Balas appointed Jonathan as high priest. The acceptance of this act indicates that by this time both the Maccabees and the Jewish community in general granted the right to make this appointment to the suzerain of the empire.

This was quite ironic. One of the roots of the entire Maccabean revolt had been the resistance of the Jewish community to the appointment of high priests by Antiochus IV Epiphanes. Yet here was one of those same Maccabees seeking to bring the revolt to an end by accepting the appointment as high priest from a man who claimed to be the surviving son of that same Antiochus.

As a result of the concessions, Jonathan had a fairly independent hand in Jerusalem. He began to rebuild both the city and the Temple wall in Jerusalem. Further, as a part of the concessions made by Demetrius earlier, many of the Syrian garrisons which had been established in Judea were evacuated. This may also have been done because Demetrius I needed the troops. Only Beth-zur and the Acra were left defended.

Following the defeat of Demetrius I in 150 BC, Alexander Balas had been installed as king at Ptolemais, where the wedding with Cleopatra was held. Jonathan was present, and there he was reconfirmed as high priest, elevated to "First Friend of the King," and appointed governor of the province of Judea. Now, instead of being a rebel and commander of insurrectionists, he was the official representative of the Seleucid empire. In him were now combined the political, religious, and military authority of the region. What a change had transpired from those first days of rebellion in Modein seventeen years earlier.

In the next five years (150-145 BC), Jonathan consolidated his position in Judea and Jerusalem. He was opposed in Jerusalem by some of the orthodox Jews because, although he was from a priestly family, he was not of the line of Zadok. At the same time, his leadership was welcomed by most Jews, for it brought a period of relative peace and stability, as well as a certain degree of prominence to their region. His positive relationship with Alexander Balas brought an increase in the territory over which he ruled, giving him authority over much of the coastal plain. At the invasion of Demetrius II in Phoenicia, Ptolemy VI of Egypt sought, apparently, to come to the aid of his son-in-law, Alexander Balas. As he marched northward along the coastal highway, he was escorted by Jonathan as the governor of the region.

Once Ptolemy VI crossed into Syria proper, Jonathan returned to Jerusalem. He used the war between Alexander Balas and Demetrius II as a cover for attacking the Acra in Jerusalem. Assuming, rightly, that the demands of the civil war would keep either combatant from interfering, Jonathan besieged the Syrian garrison there. As we have seen, however, the Syrian civil war was over quickly, and Demetrius II was left in absolute control. The Jerusalem Hellenists immediately appealed for help, and Jonathan was summoned to Ptolemais to give an accounting to Demetrius II.

Two factors came into play at that point. First, Jonathan was master of the art of political diplomacy. Second, Demetrius recognized Jonathan's ability and power. Needing friends more than enemies, Demetrius II reaffirmed Jonathan as both high priest and governor. The Jewish leader was named to the order of "First Friends" of Demetrius, even as he had been for Demetrius's predecessor. Jonathan was also given part, if not all, of the province of Samaria. Some reduction in taxes was also made. On the other hand, he did have to give up his attack on the Acra and agree to Syrian garrisons remaining there and at Beth-zur.

Shortly thereafter an uprising in Antioch threatened the rule of Demetrius, and he sent to Jonathan for aid. The Hebrew leader sent three thousand troops to the king's aid, quickly quelling the revolt. However, Jonathan was not given the rewards he thought was due for this aid. Thus some of his loyalty to Demetrius II was forfeited.

In the ensuing conflict between Trypho, in the name of Antiochus VI, and Demetrius II, Jonathan traded his allegiance to Trypho for additional concessions. He was given additional territory to govern, and Simon, his brother, was named military commander of the entire coastal region. Simon's military activities for Trypho were more successful than Jonathan's. Trypho with their support gained control of most of the western part of the empire, including Antioch.

Then Trypho had the boy-prince assassinated and seized the throne for himself (142 BC). This forced him to consolidate his hold on the western part of the Seleucid kingdom. Jonathan used this period as an opportunity to try to consolidate his own hold on Judea. Jonathan finally occupied the Acra, and Simon overcame Beth-zur (ca. 143/142 BC). Thus, at long last, no Syrian garrisons remained in Judea. The Acra, however, was apparently reoccupied by the Syrians shortly thereafter.

Once Trypho was relatively secure, he realized that he had to deal with the Maccabees. He marched southward and was met by Jonathan and his troops at Scythopolis. A battle was avoided, and Jonathan agreed to go with Trypho to Ptolemais for diplomatic talks. At that time, Jonathan was arrested and held in bondage. Simon, in turn, assumed the leadership of the Maccabean forces and took the position of high priest. Just prior to his arrest, Jonathan had been in negotiations with both Rome and Sparta. He was a man of diplomatic significance and was so recognized. Even though these two powers had ulterior reasons for creating problems for the Seleucids, they did not negotiate with nonentities.

When Simon became leader in Jerusalem, he completed the rebuilding of the walls of Jerusalem which Jonathan had begun. Trypho then began an advance into Judea and was met by Simon at Adida, a fortress on the road from Joppa to Jerusalem. Trypho insisted that he was holding Jonathan as hostage for payment of taxes owed to the government. Under no real illusions, Simon paid the ransom, but Jonathan was not released. Trypho sought to circle southward and attack Jerusalem through Idumea. However, a snowstorm turned him back. It was then that Trypho turned homeward. Passing through Gilead, at a place called Baskama, Jonathan was executed in 142 BC. No reason was given for that traitorous act.

With the death of Jonathan and the accession of Simon to full and independent leadership, a new era had come for Judea. Most historians agree that Simon was the first truly independent ruler of the Hasmonean kingdom. That is so. But beyond any question, it was the political diplomacy of Jonathan which made the whole thing possible.

The Consequences of the Maccabean Revolt

In assessing the significant consequences of any period of history, two major difficulties confront the historian. First, it is always difficult to say what would or might have resulted from the same era if the events of the period had not occurred and other events had happened. Thus, in assessing such an era, all that we can say is what visible and measurable changes did occur from the beginning to the end. We can only assume that the changes were the result of the events. In some instances, it may have been the other way around; the events may have happened because the changes were occurring. The second difficulty which must be considered is that is easy to disagree on what real change took place in any given era. This is especially so when that era is as brief as the twenty-five years of the period of the Maccabean Revolt (167-142 BC). Therefore, with no illusions about the fact that significant disagreements exist as to the ultimate consequences of the Maccabean Revolt, I would like to suggest that the following appear to be worth noting.

Social and Economic Changes

Prior to this era, the main unrest of the people of Jerusalem and Judea had been among the wealthy and the powerful. In the Maccabean Revolt, however, the common people had found a cause and a voice. Further, they had also discovered that there is a power which ordinary people can wield over world empires and their rulers. More than any other time of the interbiblical period, this was a time of social upheaval when those normally in power discovered their power flowing away from them.

Economically, the constant conflict of the period had to be a drain upon the wealth and the resources of the nation. On the other hand, the massive drain of tribute to foreign potentates was significantly reduced. The laborers and small landholders appear to have been somewhat better off at the end of the revolt than they were at the beginning. On the other hand, those people of major wealth who had prospered under the status quo and the Hellenizing of the land suffered significantly from the revolt. The sources of their income, the trade, the control of taxation, and the control of the Temple all dried up. It was a time of the resurgence of the middle and lower classes.

Religious Changes

Without question, the most significant changes of the era were in the area of religion. The most significant among these was religious freedom.

At the beginning of the period, the worship of Yahweh was all but illegal. The traditional and characteristic practices of Judaism had been illegal and disobedience was punishable by death. Pagan worship was required of all people. By the end, however, full religious freedom was restored. The people could worship according to the Torah and that right was guaranteed to them by the civil government.

In addition to that fundamental change, a new feast of joy had been added to the Jewish religious calendar. Hanukkah, or the Feast of Lights, was an eight-day celebration which was to be held annually to commemorate the rededication of the Temple. New religious celebrations come about very infrequently. Here is one in which the early days of the revolt have been remembered and celebrated for more than twenty centuries.

Also, in this period a theological belief reached full development: the idea of life after death. The growing faith in life after death significantly affected the attitude toward both death and life. This new dimension of faith did not sweep away all opposition. The disagreement on this issue between the Pharisees and the Sadducees in Jesus' day clearly illustrates this. However, as the people began to realize that there is more to human experience than this life only, they then faced the issues of death and suffering differently. People were more willing to die for their faith when they believed that their real life with God did not end with physical death.

Literary Developments

It has long been recognized that the era prior to and during the Maccabean Revolt was the most fertile for the development of apocalyptic literature. No real agreement exists as to when or how apocalyptic literature developed in the Hebrew tradition. No disagreement exists as to the fact that this literary form flourished most fully during the days, particularly the early days, of the Maccabees.

Apocalyptic literature is designed to encourage people facing intense national and personal crises because of godless foreign powers. Resting in the absolute sovereignty of God, this literature is intended to produce hope and confidence in the ultimate victory of God when His people are facing catastrophic times.

The time of the Maccabees was more one of military action rather than literary activity. The major exception appears to be the work of the apocalyptists. To think of apocalyptic literature is to think of the Maccabean era. Other times produced their apocalypses, but none was so fruitful as this.

Political Changes

The final major consequence of the Maccabean era was political. The Hebrew people were more politically independent by the end of Jonathan's life (142 BC) than they had been since Jerusalem fell to Babylon (586 BC). At the outset, the goal of the revolt was religious freedom. However, somewhere very early in the period, the goal of political independence was added. It remained for Judas's military accomplishments and Jonathan's political diplomacy to transform the dream into reality. When Simon assumed the leadership, for the first time in more than four centuries, foreign control was absent from the territory of Judea. The wind of freedom flowed through the land and the breath of freedom was breathed by all the people. Judea was never the same again.

The Rise of Political and Religious Groups

In many ways, the twenty-five year period of the Maccabean Revolt was one of the most fertile for the development of all phases of Jewish life. Among the many facets of Jewish national life which took shape, at least in formative stages, during this time were the numerous religious and political parties which were active for the next two or three centuries. It is significant, perhaps, that the era began with the essential demise of the two parties which had been quite active for almost a century, the Oniads and the Tobiads. As we have seen, these two families (parties) struggled with one another over the issue of authority in Jerusalem and in Judaism. However, they were both representative of the wealthy leaders of Jerusalem. They showed little concern for and had little or no support from the people of the land. Through the high priesthood of Jason and Menelaus, the Tobiads apparently had the upper hand. But with the death of Menelaus and the rise of popular revolt, the influence of both families ceased to be a significant factor in the life of the Hebrew people. But others took their places.

The Hellenists

The Hellenists arose among the Jews long prior to this period. The Tobiads were a part of the Hellenists, but were not the only part. This group had no necessary intent to be apostates. They did intend to be unorthodox. They were seeking a good life and were willing to experiment with new ideas and new ways. As the hatred of the orthodox solidified, these people began to hate in return. Violence was shown by both sides, and the end result was that they were driven into apostasy by those who were the defenders of orthodoxy. During the revolt, they became supporters of the foreign conquerors and were treated with brutality by the "defenders of the faith."

The Maccabeans or Hasmoneans

Obviously the Maccabeans were the leaders of the revolt. But their followers were the people of the land who would yield no further to the demands of foreign conquerors. To them, there were issues which were more important than life itself. They were willing to suffer, to risk everything, and to die to show how important their faith and the Torah was to them. The larger body of Maccabeans was apparently made up of at least three groups. First were those who sought religious freedom for themselves. They insisted upon the right to worship God in their own way. They refused to worship any other god or in any other manner. Faith was more important than life itself. The second group also sought religious freedom, but to that goal they added, if they did not hold it at first, the goal of political freedom. The family of the Hasmoneans themselves became a part of this group. Nothing would be sufficient until every foreign soldier was withdrawn from the land which God had given them. After religious freedom had been attained, these two groups fell out with one another because their ultimate goals differed.

The third group among the Maccabees were simply the disaffected. These are present in every movement of revolution. They were simply striking out at life as it was. They seemed simply to be motivated with the desire for change, believing that anything must be better than things as they were. They are also seekers after power. Having been oppressed by others, they sought to do some oppressing of their own. The latter two groups continued the struggle after the departure of the first from their ranks.

The Hasidim

The Hasidim (or Hasadeans, as they are sometimes called) were "the pious ones." Their name is tied in with and derived from the Old Testament term *hesedh,* which refers to covenant loyalty. This concept truly underlay their self-understanding. These were the backbone of the faithful who considered that loyalty to the covenant of God and to the God of the covenant was the most important issue in anyone's life. Their concern was not only with obedience to the Torah but ultimately with rooting out all disobedience in Judaism. They were early supporters of the Maccabees, but later many of them separated from it because of what they viewed as religious compromise. To them, that was the ultimate in evil. For good people to compromise with the forces of evil was viewed as worse than the evil forces themselves. Thus their hatred of the disloyal among Hebrews knew no limits.

The Sadducees

The Sadducees really do not appear in this period, but their roots are to be found here. First of all, in the New Testament era they clearly did not believe in the resurrection of the dead. We have noted that the resurrection hope came into its own in the early days of the Jewish revolt. Some of those who did not accept this view were among the ancestors of the Sadducees. Further, they were generally the wealthy aristocracy, including priests, merchants, and government leaders. In a sense, the Tobiads also were a part of their heritage. These people were concerned with maintaining things as they were, for in that situation they had wealth, prominence, and power. They were supporters of the status quo who opposed anything which threatened or lessened their power and position. Their party had more of a social background than anything else.

The Pharisees

According to Josephus (in at least one reference), the Pharisees showed up for the first time in the period of Jonathan's leadership. Elsewhere, he located their origin somewhat later. The point is that there is no clear-cut time when they can be said to begin to be present in Jewish life. Because of the scathing denunciation of them in the New Testament, they have been grossly misunderstood. They are truly descendants of the Hasidim, and their primary concern was in keeping faith with God. To them, this meant keeping the Law, the whole Law. They, in many instances, went to what some consider to have been ridiculous extremes in seeking to help people do this. But we must acknowledge that they were probably among some of the best people the world has ever known. They did not seek to make the Law a burden. Rather, they sought to make life meaningful and livable. They wanted above everything else to do what God wanted, precisely what God wanted, and only what God wanted. Unfortunately they became so convinced that they were the only true defenders of the faith that they became harsh and judgmental in their relationship with others. We need to remember that Jesus did not condemn them for keeping the Law. Instead, He commended them for it. What He did condemn them for was their alienation of others and their lack of compassion.

The Essenes

The Essenes are a lesser-known sect of Judaism. Their origin is unsure, although prevailing opinion ties them originally to the Hasidim. They were primarily an ascetic sect, living to themselves. There were small enclaves in several cities of Palestine, but a major group is said to have lived above the Dead Sea. They were concerned with a thorough understanding of and preservation of the Scriptures. They were also considered to be connected with a group of healers, whose prime concern was not only a healthy spirit but a healthy body as well. They were pacifists and kept no slaves. They were also celibate. Thus their ranks had to be filled with converts, not with births. They are said by Josephus to have been in existence by the time of Jonathan. Their emphasis upon strict sabbath observance coupled with their pacifism make them likely descendants of the nonmilitant side of the Hasidim.

The Qumran Community

This group was unknown until the discovery of the Dead Sea scrolls. This group appears to have been largely priestly, calling themselves the sons of Zadok. This may be more of a nickname than an actual heritage. Many of their beliefs have caused people to identify them with Essenes. They also called themselves the Covenanters. Many of their beliefs were similar to those of the Pharisees. Identification is as yet unsure, but it appears most likely that they were a branch of the Essenes, if not the mainstream. They did spend a major portion of their time in the study and preservation of the Scriptures. Because of this, with the finding of much of their library, our knowledge of much of the Old Testament Hebrew text was moved back in time by almost a thousand years. Since we know nothing about them outside of their own writings, they apparently were well outside the mainstream of Jewish life.

The Nationalists, the Zealots

Most readers are familiar with the Zealots from New Testament times. Even one of the apostles was of that group. These were people dedicated to the driving out of any foreign ruler and every foreign soldier. Prior to the time of Alexander, the Jews apparently were content to dwell under Persian domination. However, with the rise of Hellenism, a new day dawned. It came to a head in the revolt of Mattathias and his sons. From that time onward, there was always a group in Israel who would be satisfied with nothing less than absolute victory over the foreign powers who oppressed them. This was perceived of in terms of a crusade, fulfilling the purpose of Yahweh, the God of Israel. This group put their lives on the line again and again until finally the last soldiers of the Seleucids was driven forth. They later resisted every renewed effort at occupation or domination. Their motto seems to have simply been "live free or die." Nothing else was sufficient.

It is worthy of note that with the exception of the Hellenists and the Sadducees, the major emphasis of all of these parties was the freedom to serve God as their fathers had. They sought to follow the law, to keep their covenant commitments. Major differences separated them in belief. But loyalty to their God bound them together. That was the legacy the Maccabean Revolt left to Israel. Her people have seldom departed from that faith.

6
The Hasmonean Period
(142-63 BC)

With the death of Jonathan (142 BC), the situation in Judea changed both rapidly and radically. Upon the succession of his brother Simon to leadership, conditions changed enough that we seek to indicate that difference by no longer referring to the Maccabees but to the Hasmoneans. The time of the Maccabean Revolt was one of constant turmoil and upheaval. Instability and uncertainty were the order of the day. However, with Simon and his successors, an hereditary line was set up which at least gave an appearance of stability to the nation (province) of Judea. This was the Hebrews' last chance at independence until modern times.

Chronological Table
The Hasmonean Period (142-63 BC)

Egypt	*Syria*	*Jerusalem and Judea*
Ptolemy VIII (145-116)	Demetrius II (145-139)	Simon (142-135/34)
	Trypho (142-138)	
	Demetrius captive in Parthia (139-128)	
	Antiochus VII (138-128)	John Hyrcanus (135/34-104)
	Campaigns in Judea, Samaria, and Idumea	
	Demetrius II (128-125)	

		Antiochus VIII (125-113)
		Antiochus IX (113-95)

Conquest of Iturea

Conquest of Samaria
and Idumea

Ptolemy IX (116-107)

Cleopatra III (107-101)   Aristobulus I (104-103)

Alexander Jannaeus
(103-76)

Ptolemy X   Demetrius III
(101-88)   (95-87)   Coastal Plain captured
(ca. 95)

Civil war (ca. 88)

Antiochus XII
(86-84)

Salome Alexandra
(76-67)
Hyrcanus II, high
priest (76-67)

Syria made a   Aristobulus II (67-63)
Roman province
(64)

Pompey conquers
Jerusalem (63)

The Priestly Rule

The International Scene

At the time of the death of Jonathan, the Syrian empire was being torn by the civil war between Demetrius II and Trypho, who called himself king after the murder of the young Antiochus VI. During this time of turmoil, the Parthians to the east made major inroads into the Seleucid territories. At that point, 141 BC, Demetrius II marched eastward to deal with that threat. He apparently planned on strengthening his hold on the east in order better to deal with Trypho's threat in the south and west.

Regardless of his plans, they all came to nought, for Demetrius was captured about 139 BC by the Parthians. Unlike many other rulers and their captives, the Parthian King Mithridates I neither executed nor abused Demetrius II. He did keep him in close captivity, but he was honored as a king. However, the captivity of Demetrius gave Trypho the opportunity which he had been seeking. He was now sole king over Syria. He was also the first Syrian king not of the Seleucid line. The coins which he minted indicate that he envisioned himself as the founder of a new empire, and its dates started with his own accession. However, that was both premature and very insecure.

Two events followed upon one another which were to spell the downfall of Trypho. Demetrius II, the captured king, had a brother, Antiochus, who had been living for a time in Asia Minor. When he learned of his brother's captivity and of the activity of Trypho, he gathered a mercenary army and marched into the region of Syria. In the meantime, some of Trypho's troops, disturbed by his high-handed policies both toward the boy-king, Antiochus VI and toward the captive Demetrius II, deserted to Demetrius's wife Cleopatra Thea. We have no way of knowing if they were wholly altruistic in this or if Cleopatra had made some sort of offer or concession to them.

At this point, Cleopatra, living in Seleucia, offered to marry Antiochus in order to legitimize his claim to the throne of his imprisoned brother. He did so and began to reign in the place of his captive brother as Antiochus VII Sidetes. This marriage meant that Cleopatra Thea had been married to three Seleucid kings, Alexander Balas, Demetrius II, and now Antiochus VII. Their combined forces now pursued Trypho throughout the land, until he was finally captured. Shortly thereafter, Trypho committed suicide (138 BC), probably under duress.

Not long after his consolidation of control in Syria, Antiochus VII sought to regain control of Judea, or at least of parts of it. When his diplomatic advances were rebuffed, he moved militarily against the Jews under Simon, but was thoroughly defeated, and the issue was dropped for a while. However, in 135/34 BC, Antiochus made another invasion into Judea. This one was better organized and better supplied. It was also a much larger force. This invasion thoroughly decimated the land of

Judea and the new leader of the Jews, John Hyrcanus, was besieged in Jerusalem. When the situation became desperate, the Jews surrendered. In spite of advice to thoroughly destroy the city, Antiochus Sidetes dealt with them generously. Whether he did this because of his nature, because he needed the support of John Hyrcanus in his battles against the Parthians, or because of the threat of Rome, we do not know. Each of these reasons can be supported with some evidence. At this point, though, it is inconclusive. I assume that the Roman threat was the more likely reason.

In 130 BC, Antiochus marched eastward to attack the Parthians. At this threat, the Parthians released Demetrius II in order to create problems for the Seleucids. This they certainly did, for the Seleucid empire was once again blessed (or cursed) with two living claimants to the throne. Forces of Jews under John Hyrcanus marched with Antiochus on his campaign to the east. The Syrian troops were at first victorious, but in 129 BC, Antiochus VII Sidetes was killed in battle and the attack of the Syrians collapsed.

Demetrius II was once again the undisputed king of Syria. Needing to gain a firm control over his kingdom, he did not have an opportunity to deal in any way with John Hyrcanus. Almost immediately, Demetrius II had an argument with his brother-in-law, apparently over the situation of Cleopatra. Ptolemy VIII sent a rival claimant to the throne of Syria into the land, one Alexander Zabinas, supposedly a son of Alexander Balas. Demetrius II was defeated at a battle near Damascus. Fleeing to Ptolemais and then to Tyre, he was assassinated there about 126 BC.

Alexander Zabinas sought to take firm control, but was prevented by the son of Demetrius II, Antiochus Grypus. They fought for a few years, but Alexander was taken captive in 123/22 BC, and shortly thereafter was executed. Demetrius's son was now able to reign as undisputed king under the name of Antiochus VIII. He was able to reign in peace for only a few years, however. Sometime thereafter, the step-brother of the king, another son of Demetrius, Antiochus Kysikenos, laid claim to the throne. They fought periodically until about 113 BC, when Antiochus IX Kysikenos got the upper hand. Antiochus VIII disappears from the scene, and we hear nothing else about him for a number of years, when Josephus tells of his death.

This constant inner conflict had seriously weakened the Seleucid power. When shortly thereafter, John Hyrcanus besieged Samaria, the Samaritans appealed to Antiochus IX for aid. He sought to come to their aid, but was utterly unsuccessful. He formed an alliance with the Egyptians but, after some inconsequential victories, was forced to retire in defeat. The once mighty Seleucid empire had come upon dismal times. The constant conflict over the throne had destroyed its place as a world power. For this development, the Jews in Jerusalem had every reason to give thanks.

Simon (142-135/34 BC)

When Jonathan was arrested and finally murdered by Trypho (142 BC), Simon assumed the leadership of the Maccabean forces. He was the last surviving son of Mattathias, whose acts had initiated the revolt. Simon appears to have coupled the military skills of Judas with the diplomatic abilities of Jonathan.

Taking advantage of the ongoing conflict between Trypho and Demetrius II, Simon entered into negotiation with Demetrius. Demetrius needed the Jewish support in his conflict with Trypho, and Simon made good use of his position. The Syrian king agreed to remove all demands for taxation from Judea and Jerusalem. At that point, Judea became an independent state. The edict of Demetrius II is dated in May, 142 BC. Simon had secured in the first days of his leadership what Mattathias had dreamed of, what Judas had struggled for, and what Jonathan had moved toward through diplomacy. At that time, the Seleucid calendar was abolished and a Jewish one was adopted, beginning with the first year of Simon. First Maccabees sums it up quite succinctly. "In [that] . . . year the yoke of the Gentiles was removed from Israel" (1 Macc. 13:41, RSV).

Simon was given a time of respite from foreign interference due to the ongoing conflict between Trypho and Demetrius II. Further, the Parthian pressure took Demetrius eastward in 141 BC. This allowed Simon ample time for all sorts of steps to consolidate both his position and the military and economic situation in Jerusalem and Judea.

In September 140 BC, a great assembly was held in Jerusalem. It had a twofold purpose. First, the assembly was intended as a celebration and thanksgiving to God for His deliverance. This was important for all the people. The second reason for the assembly was more important to Simon, however, for that was to elect him high priest.

Ever since the time of Antiochus IV Epiphanes, the Jewish high priest had held his position by virtue of his appointment by a foreign, pagan king. This had begun with Antiochus's appointment of Jason in 175 BC. Thirty-four years later, the Jewish people named their own high priest. That was for them, the ultimate mark of independence.

However, the election of Simon as high priest posed some problems. As we have noted before, the Maccabees, while being descended from Aaron (and, therefore, legitimate priests), were not descended from Zadok. Zadok became high priest under Solomon and his descendants had held the high-priestly office until Antiochus IV Epiphanes had appointed Menelaus and deposed Jason (172 BC). The Hasidim still believed that only Zadokites could be high priests.

When Jason had been appointed high priest, Menelaus, the son of the incumbent Onias III had fled Judea and ultimately had gone to Egypt where he had built a temple in Leontopolis. We know little of this except that it survived and was actively used by some Egyptian Jews for a number of years. However, this meant that the "official" high-priestly line was no longer available in Jerusalem. Yet the Hasidim would not agree to a permanent appointment to the high priesthood for a non-Zadokite family. A compromise was reached and Simon was made high priest forever "until there should arise a prophet of credance" (1 Macc. 14:41). This allowed Simon and his descendants to have an hereditary priesthood until the Lord should raise up His own man to fill the office. By this means, the pious ones managed to accept a non-Zadokite high priest elected by the people until God should provide a different one.

Simon had inherited from his brother the position of military leader, provincial governor, and high priest. That high priesthood had been at the discretion of a foreign ruler, however, and that was no longer tenable for an independent state. After the popular election of the assembly in Jerusalem, Simon was high priest, ethnarch (governor), and commander-in-chief of the army. He was high priest and from that position ruled over the entire nation. Further, by being elected "forever," he had established a dynastic rule over the land. He was to take advantage of that authority and position immediately.

Even before the Acra fell, Simon had attacked and captured Gazara (ancient Gezer) which controlled the access route from Joppa to Jerusalem. Simon also entered into negotiations with Rome, apparently establishing a treaty with them which guaranteed the independence of Judea.

At this point, Demetrius II was captured by the Parthians (ca. 138 BC). It appeared, as we have seen, that Trypho was now the undisputed leader of Syria. However, Antiochus VII Sidetes invaded and defeated Trypho. Simon entered into negotiations with Antiochus VII and received another right which further undergirded his independence, the right of coining money. However, to this time, archaeologists have not found any coins which can be dated to this time with certainty. Some coins, with the inscription, "Simeon, prince of Israel," once dated to this era are now assigned to the time of the last Jewish revolt, about AD 132-135. On the other hand, some scholars believe that coins inscribed "Jerusalem the Holy" and on the other side "Shekel of Israel" may belong to the time of Simon. The issue is unclear and uncertain. Even if there are such coins, they would only have been accepted in Jewish territory.

Clearly Antiochus VII Sidetes did not wholly recognize Jewish independence. When he had defeated Trypho, he decided to settle affairs with Judea. He ordered Simon to surrender the Acra, Gazara, Joppa, and all other fortified cities which the Jews had occupied or to pay a penalty of five hundred talents. Simon claimed these sites belonged to the Jews originally and had been occupied by the Gentiles only temporarily. Simon did offer one hundred talents as payment for the problems created by his warfare.

Insulted by the effrontery of what he considered a rebel, Antiochus Sidetes ordered the governor of the coastal regions, Cendebaeus to attack Simon and drive him out. Simon, too old to be involved in active campaigns, appointed his two sons, John and Judas, military commanders. They met Cendebaeus at Azotus (ancient Ashdod) and thoroughly defeated him. So overwhelming was this defeat that Judea was left in peace for the remainder of Simon's life.

That, however, was not to be long. Simon had a son-in-law by the name of Ptolemy who had a fortress at Dok (the modern *'ain Duk*), about four miles northwest of Jericho. In early 135/34 BC, Ptolemy invited Simon to a banquet, got him drunk, and assassinated him. His intent was to seize the Hasmonean power for himself. In this he was supported by the Hellenists of the land. However, he was thwarted in those designs.

Word of the death of Simon quickly reached Simon's son John (known as John Hyrcanus) who was in Jerusalem at the time. John immediately moved to take possession of his father's chambers in the Temple. When Ptolemy's messengers arrived, they were executed by John. Then John Hyrcanus marched to Dok and besieged Ptolemy. Ptolemy, seeing that his situation was hopeless, executed John Hyrcanus's mother and two of his younger brothers who had been imprisoned when Simon was assassinated. Ptolemy then fled to Cappadocia and the coup failed, leaving John Hyrcanus firmly in control.

John Hyrcanus (135/34-104 BC)

Before he left Jerusalem, John Hyrcanus I (as he has become known) was publicly acclaimed as the lawful successor to Simon. Antiochus VII Sidetes, whose position in Syria was reasonably secure at the moment, used this time of Jewish turmoil as an opportunity to renew his attack upon Judea. In John's first year, Antiochus VII marched into Palestine. His armies quickly overcame the land, and John Hyrcanus was besieged in Jerusalem. After a year, imminent starvation finally forced John to surrender.

At this point, Antiochus VII Sidetes showed magnimity to his defeated enemies. Against the advice of his councillors, he did not destroy Jerusalem. Rather, he demanded the renewal of tribute payments, the payment of five hundred talents indemnity for the conquest of Joppa and Gazara, the release of all prisoners, and the destruction of the walls of Jerusalem. The internal administration of the affairs of Judea were left in John's hands. Further, Antiochus allowed Temple worship to continue and gave magnificent offerings himself. So gracious and generous was he that the Jews called him Antiochus the Pious. His generous terms to John Hyrcanus also won his friendship, at least openly. However, behind the scenes, John Hyrcanus entered into negotiations with the Parthians against Antiochus.

In 130 BC, Antiochus VII marched toward Parthia to renew his claims there. John marched with him. At that time, however, perhaps as a result of the negotiations of John Hyrcanus, the Parthians released their long-held captive, Demetrius II. Once again Syria had two kings. That didn't last long. Antiochus VII Sidetes was killed in battle in 129 BC. John returned home with no opposition. Once again, he established Jewish independence. This time, the Seleucid control was gone forever.

Upon his return to Jerusalem, John Hyrcanus sought to consolidate his position and win support of all the people. He did this by having a great banquet for all the elders, assuring them of his commitment to the Torah. He also urged all of them to let him know if he ever violated any part of the law or tradition. At this point, an elder of the Hasidim or Pharisees urged him to resign the high priesthood. The reason for this was a rumor that shortly before his birth, his mother had been a prisoner of the Seleucids. This put his legitimacy in question. John was so enraged at this that he dismissed the guests and ended the banquet. This created a break between the Hasmoneans and the Pharisees which never healed. That animosity, however, won the friendship of the Sadducees. This breach never healed and troubled the nation for the rest of its history. With the growing weakness of the Syrians, John Hyrcanus began a time of territorial expansion. He took over the Samaritans to the north, capturing their capital at Shechem and destroying the rival temple on Mount Gerizim. This put the final brick in the wall of separation and hatred between Israel's two people.

During Hyrcanus's siege of Shechem, the inhabitants appealed to Antiochus IX, king of Syria. He attacked the Jewish forces but was beaten decisively. When Shechem fell, Hyrcanus utterly leveled the city. He then extended his northern conquests as far as Scythopolis (Bethshan). To the south, he overcame longtime enemies in Idumea (Edom), forcing them to become Jews and be circumcised. However, the orthodox Jews of Jerusalem never considered them to be full Jews. This was to create problems later with Herod. As an Idumean, he considered himself a Jew, but the Pharisees did not. John Hyrcanus also expanded his territorial control in the Transjordan.

By about 128 BC (some historians think it was somewhat later), John Hyrcanus had expanded his territorial holdings in all directions. The land area over which he ruled was roughly equivalent to that ruled over by David at the time of his death. Although John Hyrcanus was high priest of Jerusalem, he apparently saw himself primarily as a secular ruler. He did not even bother to use a Jewish army but primarily used mercenaries for troops, paid for by the taxes which he collected as high priest.

Internationally, Hyrcanus maintained good relationships with Rome and instituted such with Egypt. These had the double purpose of keeping Syria at bay and securing independence and support for Hyrcanus.

Internally, Hyrcanus almost certainly minted some Judean coins. A great many have been found with his name upon them. Many of these may come from his reign. John Hyrcanus had a major need for funds to pay his mercenaries. The sources of revenue for such ambitious enterprises were not sufficient. Thus, he began plundering tombs, like others before him, especially of foreign kings. He even plundered the tomb of David. This created great hostility on the part of many of the orthodox. The break with the Pharisees was solidified at this point.

Further, numerous indications survive which imply that John Hyrcanus wished to be king of Judea. That, however, was denied him. As a descendant of Aaron, he had a legitimate claim upon the priesthood, even though he wasn't a Zadokite. He could in no way, however, establish a legitimate claim upon the kingship, for he was not of the house of

David. His desire for this honor and power clearly added further fuel to the Pharisaic hatred for him. This, in turn, further exacerbated the division between the Pharisees and the Hasmoneans and strengthened their growing ties with the Sadducees. Regardless of his desires, John was forced by what he perceived to be public opinion to continue to call himself ethnarch instead of king.

The Kingly Rule

The International Scene

Only one force of major significance for understanding the events in Judea exists in the era from 104-63 BC. That is Rome. Syria had generally ceased to be a significant threat. Egypt still sought to have some influence, but it was relatively unimportant. Rome was another matter.

We have seen throughout our study the growing influence of Rome in affairs in the eastern end of the Mediterranean. This begins primarily with the defeat of Hannibal's Carthaginian army about 202 BC. Because of Macedonian support for Hannibal, Rome became involved with Greece and Macedon. Because of the attacks of Antiochus III on Greece in 192 BC, Rome attacked and defeated him at Magnesia and followed that with the peace treaty of Apamea (188 BC). The financial burdens of this treaty shaped Syrian policy for years. In 165 BC, the mere message of a Roman emissary turned the forces of Antiochus IV Epiphanes back from Egypt, starting the entire train of events which led to the Maccabean Revolt. Further, the Maccabean leaders, whenever possible, sought to undergird their position with support from Rome in the way of treaties.

In 146 BC, Rome moved into the Balkan peninsula, following an uprising in Greece. The revolt was crushed, and two new provinces were added to the empire, Macedonia in the north and Achaia to the south. Upon the death of the king of Pergamum in 133 BC, the province of Asia was added, the first Roman province on the Asian continent. To the northeast of this region, Mithridates IV of the Arsacid dynasty, made an attempt to establish an Asian empire, attacking in 88 BC. No question exists as to his skill, both as a military leader and as a master of the art of propaganda. However, he was aided when civil war in Rome and a slave rebellion in both Italy and Spain began in 74 BC. The war with Mithridates dragged on for twenty-five years. Pompey, a general of Rome, was given responsibility for the war in 66 BC. In one major campaign, he drove Mithridates totally from the region. He fled to the Black Sea and committed suicide in 63 BC.

Pompey was suddenly faced with the entire region of Asia-Syria-Palestine which was in a chaotic state. A preliminary march into Syria by Scaurus, Pompey's lieutenant, settled nothing. In 63 BC, Pompey arrived in Damascus. Two rival claimants to the Hasmonean throne sought his support. In addition, a delegation (Pharisees?) from Jerusalem urged him to abolish the Hasmonean monarchy. The end result of this appeal was a Roman campaign into Judea and the capture of the Temple in 63 BC. At that point, Judea came under the control of the most powerful and ruthless empire the world had ever known.

Aristobulus I (104-103 BC)

The corrupting power of power itself is seen most vividly in the brief reign of Hyrcanus's son, Aristobulus I. John Hyrcanus, with a long and generally successful reign behind him, sought to make provisions for his accomplishments to continue. He intended that the political and religious authority be divided after his death, with his oldest son Aristobulus succeeding him as high priest and his widow assuming the reins of government. Aristobulus, however, had his mother and all of his brothers but one put in prison. The one who was not imprisoned was Antigonus, whom Aristobulus named as coregent with himself. Aristobulus had his mother starved to death in prison. Further, Salome Alexandra, his wife, and others of the court convinced him that Antigonus was a traitor, so Aristobulus had him executed. This so grieved him that it hastened his early death.

Aristobulus did what his father did not do. He took the title of king, the first Hasmonean to be so called. As a matter of policy, he used his Jewish name (Judah) at home and emphasized that he was high priest. He expanded his kingdom to the north, taking Iturea, including the northern part of Galilee. He forced the Gentiles and the Jews there who had not observed the ritual to be circumcised. This conquest of Galilee set the stage for the Galilean emphasis and concerns of the New Testament. He is remembered as being a Hellenizing ruler, but his Judaizing of Galilee was to be the most important thing he did. Aristobulus I died after a reign of only one year. His death was brought about by grief over the death of Antigonus and a disease called phthisis, a wasting disease of the lungs. Given subsequent events, it is hard not to wonder if he were possibly poisoned by his widow.

Alexander Jannaeus (103-76 BC)

The widow who survived Aristobulus I was Salome Alexandra, perhaps the most able woman in the entire interbiblical period, certainly the most outstanding among the Hasmoneans. Like most of the Hasmoneans, she bore a double name, one Jewish—Salome, one Greek—Alexandra. Her Jewish name, according to the Dead Sea Scrolls, is a contraction of *Shelom-zion,* "Peace of Zion." If ever a person was misnamed, she was. The one thing she did not bring with her was peace.

Upon the death of her husband Aristobulus, Salome freed the brothers whom he had imprisoned. She then married one of them, Alexander Jannaeus. This was legal under the Levitical code for levirate marriages, as she had borne Aristobulus no children (Deut. 25). On the other hand, this marriage showed a disregard for the law which prohibited a high priest from marrying a widow (Lev 21:14). Through the machinations of Salome, Alexander Jannaeus was both king and priest, but she appears to have been the power behind the throne for his entire reign. He blatantly called himself king in Judea.

Shortly after his accession to the throne, Alexander Jannaeus made an attack upon Ptolemais (Acco) on the coast in the northwest of Palestine. The people appealed for help to Ptolemy Lathzrus of the Egyptian royal family who was governor of Cyprus. Responding quickly, Ptolemy forced Alexander Jannaeus to raise the siege. However, Alexander plotted against Ptolemy with Cleopatra III, queen of Egypt.

When Ptolemy became aware of the treachery of Alexander Jannaeus, he raced into Galilee and overwhelmingly defeated the Jewish ruler at the Jordan. Ptolemy then proceeded down the coastal highway into Egypt. Cleopatra, in the meantime, had gathered her army and thoroughly defeated her son's troops. She pursued him almost as rapidly back up the coastal highway, forcing him to return to Cyprus. In so doing, she had occupied much of the territory of Alexander Janneus. She could have annexed Judea and many councillors advised this, but she did not. Instead, she entered into a treaty with Jannaeus. The first reason for this was the advice of Hananiah, the Jewish general of her army. He persuaded her that Judea would make a good ally. A second reason for her failure to annex Judea may have been its ties with Rome. No one in that part of the world at that time failed to take Rome seriously. Following the treaty, Cleopatra III returned to Egypt and Alexander Jannaeus was restored to his kingdom.

Alexander Jannaeus moved into new adventures. He quickly invaded

Transjordan, capturing Gadara and a few other cities. Then he invaded the Philistine plain where he captured Raphia and Gaza, among other places. By the end of this campaign (ca. 95 BC), Alexander Jannaeus had the entire coastal plain under his control with the exception of Ashkelon.

The situation at home, however, began to call for his attention. The growing opposition of the Pharisees came to a head. At a Feast of Tabernacles about 95 BC, Alexander Jannaeus deliberately poured holy water on the ground instead of on the altar. The people in the Temple threw lemons at him. He in turn had some six thousand Jews executed.

Shortly thereafter, Alexander made another attack into the Transjordan regions of ancient Moab and Ammon. This took him close to the Nabataean kingdom where his army was ambushed and almost annihilated. Alexander's flight to Jerusalem led his Jewish enemies to think he was in a particularly weak and vulnerable position. Open rebellion resulted in a civil war which lasted until about 88 BC.

Perhaps the most fascinating side of the civil war is that a Hasmonean king fought Jewish people with a mercenary army. What an ironic reversal from the Maccabean Revolt of Mattathias. We know very little of this struggle. Apparently Alexander Jannaeus held the upper hand, though only slightly. During its six-year duration about fifty thousand Jews were killed. Finally, the insurgents appealed, of all things, to a Seleucid king for help.

Demetrius III (ca. 93-87 BC) of Syria responded quickly, invading Hasmonean territory. Alexander Jannaeus was put on the defensive. He suffered a major defeat before the Seleucid army at Shechem. That defeat was actually a turning point, for the very Jews who had summoned Demetrius were now appalled at a foreign conqueror in their territory. Former opponents of Alexander Jannaeus flocked to his support. The Jewish forces were quickly able to drive the forces of Demetrius from the land. Having reestablished his authority over the kingdom, Alexander Jannaeus wreaked a horrible vengeance upon the leaders of the rebels. About eight hundred of them were arrested and were crucified in Jerusalem in full view of the palace, so that the king and his court could watch their agonies. Before the victims died, Alexander had their families brought before them and executed while the prisoners watched.

This was the man who was king in Jerusalem. Far worse, he was also high priest at the Temple of the God of Israel. This drastic and high-handed policy broke the back of any further rebellion. Alexander had no more domestic problems in his kingdom.

In its death throes, the Seleucid kingdom made one last grasp for greatness. Antiochus XII Dionysus sought to attack Aretas II of the Nabatean kingdom. In so doing, he had to pass through Hasmonean territory. Alexander sought to prevent his doing so but failed. However, in the battle against the Nabataeans, the Syrians were thoroughly defeated. That victory served as the basis of a major territorial expansion of the part of Aretas. Alexander Jannaeus was seriously threatened, but managed to get Aretas to leave Hasmonean territory in return for the restoration to Nabatean control of Alexander's Transjordan territory. Alexander, however, merely turned his attention northward. He invaded the Transjordan region of the Decapolis and overran several cities there. The inhabitants of these cities were forced to become Jews.

Ill health became the lot of Alexander Jannaeus in the latter days of his reign. However, he continued to be active militarily until the end. By the time of his death, the territory which he controlled was about the same as that which the twelve tribes had claimed at the time of the allotment under Joshua.

Prior to his death, Alexander advised his wife, Salome Alexandra, to seek peace with the Pharisees. He realized that some sort of national unity needed to be restored. He died while attacking Ragaba in 76 BC. His body was carried back to Jerusalem where he was buried with the pomp due a king and a high priest. Sadly, his long reign had been bought at an awesome price. He had sold out the best ideals of Judaism, of Hellenism, and of the Maccabeans. It may not have been visible to a contemporary, but to the historian it is obvious that the consequences of the reign of Alexander Jannaeus brought about the ultimate demise of the Hasmonean kingdom.

Salome Alexandra (76-67 BC)

Prior to his death, Alexander Jannaeus had named his wife as his successor. She had been the one behind his becoming king in the first place. During the years of his reign, Salome had either mellowed or was at least wise enough to realize that further action of the kind Alexander had pursued could only destroy her land. During the years of her reign, things were relatively quiet in Judea.

We do not know whether it was at the suggestion of Jannaeus or out of her own wisdom, but Salome took a major number of Pharisees as her advisers. It is even rumored that her brother had become a Pharisaic leader. She followed their advice so well that many of those who had been refugees returned home and those who had been imprisoned were released. However, the Pharisees began to exact such vengeance upon those who had been supporters of Alexander that the Sadducees stepped in with a plea to Salome. Those who had advised Alexander Jannaeus in his executions were themselves executed, but Salome brought the retaliations to an end.

Although Salome could and did rule, she could not serve as high priest. She associated her son, John Hyrcanus II, with her as high priest. He was a meek and mild man with no ambitions. That may have been why she selected him, as he could be so easily controlled.

Another son, Aristobulus II, was of a different temperament. He sought to be influential in matters of government and was obviously ambitious. He was a Sadducee and may have been the one who persuaded Salome to end the Pharisees' extremities. Near the end of Salome's life, he raised an army and occupied about twenty-two fortresses in Judea. We have no way of knowing what Aristobulus planned to do because at that time Salome died at seventy-three. She had shaped the course of much of the Hasmonean kingdom. She was able and ambitious and wise enough to recognize when it was time to yield to opponents and when it was safe to resist them.

Aristobulus II (67-63 BC)

Upon Salmone's death, two rival claimants were on the scene. John Hycranus II was already high priest and had the best claim to the throne. He was supported by the Pharisees. On the other hand stood Aristobulus II, supported by the powerful Sadducees, with an army in the field, and in possession of many major fortresses throughout the land.

The two forces met near Jericho, where Hyrcanus was thoroughly defeated. He fled to the Temple in Jerusalem where he surrendered to the pursuing Aristobulus. Hyrcanus had no real ambition nor little if any love for power. He apparently agreed to turn both the kingdom and the priesthood over to Aristobulus. In return, Hyrcanus was to retire, keeping his personal possessions in both land and wealth.

At this point, a man named Antipater stepped on to the stage of history. He recognized that real power is sometimes more satisfying than the trappings and appearance of power. He was an Idumean whose father (with the same name, Antipater) had served as governor of Idumea for both Alexander Jannaeus and Salome Alexandra. This son had apparently succeeded to his father's position. He took the side of Hyrcanus, leading him to make a treaty with Aretas III of the Nabateans.

The army of Aretas, along with Hyrcanus and Antipater, met and defeated Aristobulus II. He sought refuge in Jerusalem where he was besieged by Aretas. In the meantime, however, Rome had been marching into the ruins of the Seleucid empire. Both Hyrcanus II and Aristobulus II sent delegations to Damascus, asking Rome for help. Pompey sent his lieutenant, Scaurus, to investigate. When Scaurus arrived at Jerusalem, he confronted Aretas III and ordered him to return to his homeland. Unwilling to risk a war with Rome, he did just that. Scaurus returned homeward, but Aristobulus swiftly followed Aretas, attacked, and defeated him. This breach of the peace angered both Scaurus and Pompey.

Additional delegations were sent to Pompey. Along with them came a deputation of the people, probably led by Pharisees, asking Pompey to abolish the entire Hasmonean dynasty. (They knew not what they asked for!) In 63 BC, Pompey marched into Judea. Aristobulus established himself in the fortress of Alexandrium. This angered Pompey who attacked and captured Aristobulus. He then marched on Jerusalem, where Hyrcanus and his supporters opened the city to him. Some of the followers of the captive Aristobulus retreated to the Temple, where they held out for about three months. At that time, Pompey and some of his officers went into the holy of holies. That shocked the people of Jerusalem, for no one but the high priest could go in there and he only once a year, on the Day of Atonement.

Pompey then returned to Rome, carrying Aristobulus and many Jews with him as captives. These later formed the Jewish community of Rome. The kingdom of Mattathias had come to an end. The agony, the suffering, the ideals worth living and dying for had all disappeared. The kingdom had died on the altar of human ambition, sacrificed to the god of power.

The Significance of the Era

The period of the Hasmonean kingdom is one of the most action filled of any in the interbiblical period. It was a time of transition and development.

The Sadducees and the Pharisees were clearly functioning groups in the period. Their conflict with each other took significant shape and continued through the New Testament era. Both became victims of unbridled power, though the Pharisees obviously suffered the most. They were accused in New Testament times of being unloving people. The kinds of experiences which they faced under the Hasmoneans leave that kind of imprint on a society. The Pharisees of the New Testament are easier to understand having seen what they endured during this period.

Further, the Qumran community may have had its real foundation in this era. The utter disillusionment with high priests who were not worthy of the office drove many to withdraw from the official religion of Jerusalem. They simply withdrew from the life of the period and sought a way of life which allowed them to serve their God in peace. Seeing the dire wrath which was to come, they sought to study and preserve the word of the God they served.

The Jews adopted a new calendar during this era. This may seem insignificant to us, but in the ancient Near East, the use of a calendar showed where a peoples' allegiance was. Almost as much as any one thing, the dropping of the Seleucid calendar for the Hasmonean showed their independence. That was a day to be treasured, remembered, and celebrated.

Among the more major items of significance for this era were those of economics. For the first time in many centuries, the Jewish state and people were not paying tribute to a foreign power. That in itself brought a higher level of prosperity to the nation. Further, the ability to mint coins also placed Judea and Jerusalem in a place of significance on the world's marketplace. More important than any of these things, the territorial expansion of the Hasmoneans brought them control of the major highways and the coastal plain. This allowed control of trade goods. In spite of the serious consequences of all wars, the trade balance in this period had to be significantly in favor of the Hasmoneans.

But this brings us to the last issue—human suffering. It was a time when the people of Judea suffered significantly. The sadistic treatment of people by one another reveals some of the depths of human depravity. Further, the cost of war is measured not in shekels but in blood, in pain that never ends, and in the desolation of the human soul. The very things which were what the founders of the struggle lashed out against were the things which the kingdom was practicing when it came to an end.

However, above and beyond all of these features stands one consequence of the Hasmonean kingdom. We shall deal with it in all of the rest of this book. It can be summed up in one word: *Rome.*

7
Judea and the Early Roman Domination
(63-4 BC)

For most of the interbiblical period, the action was played out under the shadow of Rome. At times the shadow was more real than others, as the Peace of Apamea with the financial burdens it placed upon the Seleucid empire illustrates. At other times the shadow turned into a real presence, as when the Roman commissioner turned away Antiochus IV Epiphanes when he stood on the very verge of his long-dreamed of conquest of Egypt. But when Pompey marched into Jerusalem and seized the Temple in 63 BC, the shadow of Rome's presence became a bruising reality for the Jews of Palestine. From that point onward, the iron grasp of Rome was real. And it was stronger and more to be feared than the Ptolomies, the Seleucids, or the Hasmoneans.

Rome knew about foreign conquest. It knew that peace in a conquered territory was necessary to the collection and flow of tribute and taxes. And it also knew that the collection of taxes was the chief business of a world conqueror. Taxes flowed into the general coffers at Rome regardless of the cost in oppression to conquered peoples.

All of this, the people of Judea were to learn. They had invited Rome in. They discovered to their sorrow and regret that they could not invite Rome out.

Chronological Table
The Early Roman Period (63-4 BC)

Rome	Syria	Palestine
	Scaurus, Governor (65-62)	Hyrcanus II, high priest (63-40)
Triumvirate: Pompey, Crassus, Caesar (60-53)		

Gabinius, Governor
(57-55)   Antipater, procurator (55-43)

Crassus, Governor
(55-53)

Crassus Killed
(51)

Pompey   Cassius (53-51,
  defeated (48)   44-42)   Hyrcanus II, ethnarch (47-40)

Caesar, dictator
(45-44)

Triumvirate: Phasael, governor of Judea
  Antony, Lepidus   (ca. 43-40)
  Octavian (43-36)

                                  Herod, governor of Galilee
                                    (ca. 43-40)

                                  Antigonus, king and high priest
                                    (ca. 40-37)

                                  Herod, King (37-4)

                                            Hananel, high priest
                                              (37)
                                            Aristobulus, high
                                              priest (37)
                                            Hananel, high priest
                                              (36-30)
Octavian (Augustus)   Boethus, high priest
  sole ruler   (24-4)
  (27 BC-AD 14)

                                  Temple construction begun
                                    (ca. 20/19)

The International Scene

Prior to the actual advent of Rome, Judea was politically as well as geographically a part of the Fertile Crescent, which circled from Egypt through Palestine up through Syria and then curled over and down through the Mesopotamian Valley. With the coming of Rome from the west, however, the Parthians moved into Mesopotamia from the east. It was more than two centuries before Rome was actually able to push her frontiers into and beyond Mesopotamia. This had two major consequences for Judea. First, no longer did the land of the Jews sit in the middle of the land bridge connecting major power centers and/or major trade centers. This meant that instead of being strategically central and, therefore, strategically important, Judea was now on the frontier. Troops and trade did not pass through her borders on the way to some other place. If they came, they came specifically to be there. This took Judea out of the mainstream of international life and made it into an outpost. The second consequence derives from the first. Since Judea was no longer strategically central, a strong and able commander or governor did not need to be present in Jerusalem. That being so, the Jewish people did not receive or experience the best of Roman leadership.

Following his victory in Jerusalem in 63 BC, Pompey returned to Damascus and then went back to Rome. The next thirty to forty years were quite turbulent for Rome, for that empire was going through a metamorphosis. In 60 BC, the first Triumvirate was established. This was renewed in 56 BC over significant opposition from the Roman senate. As a consequence, the empire was ruled by Julius Caesar, Pompey, and Crassus. Caesar remained in Gaul, Pompey ruled over Spain (while remaining in Rome), and Crassus chose Syria, which included Judea.

Crassus raised funds in the winter of 54/53 BC to underwrite a campaign against the Parthians. In doing this, he plundered the treasuries of a number of temples, including the one in Jerusalem. This of course raised the ire of the Jewish people. In 51 BC, Crassus attacked the Parthians. The end result of that campaign came when he crossed the Euphrates. There his legions were soundly defeated and he was killed. News of his death sparked a revolt in Judea which was quickly ended by the action of one of Crassus's lieutenants, Cassius. He also stopped a threatened Parthian invasion in 51 BC, showing himself to be an excellent military leader.

In the meantime, divisions in Rome began to break the relationship between Pompey and Caesar. Civil war broke out between Caesar and Pompey in 49 BC. Pompey was decisively defeated at Pharsalus in Thessaly early in 48 BC. He fled to Egypt, seeking refuge. However, with

Caesar pursuing close behind, Ptolemy XIII recognized the danger and had Pompey assassinated as soon as he landed.

Caesar, upon arriving in Egypt in 48 BC, faced a conflict between Ptolemy XIII and his sister, Cleopatra. Caesar took Cleopatra's side. The forces of the boy-king Ptolemy attacked Caesar and his 3,000 soldiers, besieging them in Alexandria through the winter of 48/47 BC. Finally, aided by outside reinforcements, including Antipater of Judea, Caesar defeated the Egyptian forces, killing Ptolemy XIII, whose brother Ptolemy XIV came to the throne. However, due to Caesar's influence, the real power was exercised by Ptolemy's sister, Cleopatra. Caesar returned to Rome by way of Palestine and Asia Minor, and on the way paused at Judea to reward Antipater for his help in Egypt. Caesar arrived in Rome and became the effective dictator in 45 BC.

Cassius and Brutus, fearing the rising power of Caesar and wishing to restore the ancient traditions of the Roman republic, plotted Caesar's assassination. This was carried out on the ides of March (March 15), 44 BC. At this point, Octavian, Antony, and Lepidus formed a new Triumvirate and sought to put down the rebellion of Cassisus and Brutus. This plan was brought to a successful conclusion when the rebel forces were routed at Philippi in Macedonia in 42 BC. Brutus and Cassius committed suicide at that time. This war was costly to Judea, for Cassius sought to raise major funds from the Jews to support his cause.

The victory at Philippi left Octavian, Antony, and Lepidus in control of the Roman Empire. In the division which followed, Antony received authority over Syria, and thus over Judea. Antony went to Egypt in the winter of 41/40 BC, where he devoted his energies to Cleopatra, rather than to matters of state. His luxurious life-style increased the tax burden upon Judea.

In 40 BC, Antony made a trip back to Rome to patch up relations with Octavian, for a renewed civil war was threatened. During the absence of Antony, the Parthians invaded Roman territories in Syria. They succeeded in many areas and replaced Roman appointments with their own. Obviously Rome had to deal with this threat on the eastern edge of its empire. Herod arrived in Rome late in 40 BC. Antony and Octavian, both impressed by Herod, had nominated him to the Roman senate as king of the Jews. This was quickly confirmed. Roman election to kingship of a province was not to independence, but to the position of a dependent vassal.

At that point, Herod was a king in name only. He had to capture his kingdom. With Roman troops under his command and with others under the command of the Roman general Ventidius and his successor Sosius, the Parthians were defeated in 38 BC. However, it was not until 37 BC. that Jerusalem was recaptured for Rome.

Animosity between Octavian and Antony broke out again in 36 BC. This was instigated by Antony's marriage to Cleopatra that year. That marriage had involved a renunciation of his wife Octavia, who was the sister of Octavian. Antony first sought to drive Octavian from Rome, but failed. Octavian, on the other hand, did find a ready base of support for an expedition against Antony. The two leaders and their armies met at Actium in a sea battle, where in 31 BC Antony was defeated. He and Cleopatra fled to Egypt, and there they committed suicide.

After the death of Antony, Octavian was effectively the sole ruler of Rome and the Syrian provinces. At this point, he was given the title of Augustus, "the Exalted One." The title of *princeps civitatis,* "the first of the citizens," was also bestowed on him. This was an indication of the kind of rule he wished to establish, a type of monarchy where the emperor actually became the first of the Roman citizens. Upon the death of Lepidus (12 BC), one of the other members of the Triumvinate of Octavian, Antony, and Lepidus, Octavian truly became the sole ruler of Rome. His reign was characterized in its earlier days by territorial expansion. Although he conquered large territories in North Africa and Central Europe, he did not make any expansion to the east, in the territories of Parthia. This failure still left Judea as a frontier outpost. In his latter years he was primarily concerned with consolidation. These final days led to his rule being described as a time of peace.

The Beginning of Roman Rule

With Pompey's victory in 63 BC, Judea was made a part of the Roman province of Syria, and thus officially became a part of the Roman Empire. That meant that its fortunes were intimately tied up with Roman politics. For that to be the situation, the people of Jerusalem and Judea were led by a man extremely able to take the best advantage of those changing patterns of politics which so characterized Rome at this time.

Antipater and Hyrcanus II (63-ca. 43 BC)

We noted in the preceding chapter than Antipater was a man who sought to wield power through the manipulation of another. This he did through Hyrcanus II in the last days of the Hasmonean state. He revealed then and continued to demonstrate under Roman rule that he was a master politician. His basic policy was to maintain good relations with

Rome. He did this by openly and unreservedly supporting whomever was in power. He also kept himself (and his sons) in the limelight, making sure that both those in power and the general public saw and knew his good works. All of this kept him busy, but he accomplished it with great skill.

After Pompey's victory, Antipater sought and received the appointment of Hyrcanus II as high priest. This gave the outward appearance of at least some independence to the Jewish state. However, it was an appearance only. No real doubt existed in the minds of either the Jews or the Romans that Antipater was the actual power behind Hyrcanus. The high priest was appointed to his position by Scaurus, the governor of Syria, about 63/62 BC. The appointment was reconfirmed by Gabinius, the governor from 57-55 BC. Hyrcanus was required to pay taxes to Rome, and the non-Jewish territories won by the Hasmoneans were removed from his control.

During the early days of Roman rule, Antipater stood by Hyrcanus II. His every act was aimed at achieving the best for Judea. If it also prospered Antipater and his sons, so much the better. So loyal was he to Rome, that even when rulers changed, he was able to convince new rulers that his loyalty to their predecessors was wholly transferable.

The early days of Roman rule in Palestine were turbulent in Rome. Perhaps because of this, they were also turbulent in Judea. About 57 BC Alexander, the son of Aristobulus II who had been carried to Rome as Pompey's captive, revolted, seeking to overthrow Rome and Hyrcanus. He was wholly unsuccessful. In 56 BC, Aristobulus II and his other son, Antigonus, escaped from Rome and raised another revolt. That, too, was quickly put down. Following the defeat and death of Crassus in the battle with the Parthians in 53 BC, a third revolt was attempted by supporters of Aristobulus II, but that also was quickly ended. These three fruitless revolts cost the Jews some fifty thousand men dead or carried into captivity. Through the entire period, Antipater stood loyally with the Romans. He saw all too clearly that their ultimate victory was unquestionable. They had to maintain Judea as a part of their defense line against the Parthians to the east. In the Roman civil war between Pompey and Caesar in 49 BC, Antipater supported Pompey. Syria was his province and his generals controlled the area. However, when Caesar won at Pharsalus, Antipater immediately swung all his support to Caesar. His aid to Caesar in Egypt may even have been decisive for the Roman emperor. This had all been done in Hyrcanus's name, but everyone who mattered knew who the real power was.

On Caesar's return through Judea, the emperor paused to give his rewards for faithful support and service. Hyrcanus II was again confirmed as high priest. He was also given the title of ethnarch. As used by Caesar, this title was only slightly below king. However, as bestowed on Hyrcanus II, it was more honorary than authoritative. Far more important were the rights given to the Jews under Hyrcanus II's administration. Judaism was made a *religio licta,* a lawful religion. (This title was not actually used at this time, but the rights and privileges were the same as those granted when the Roman senate actually did use the designation in later years.) This allowed the spread of Jewish synagogues throughout the Diaspora, establishing the bases which the early Christian missionaries later sought. Taxes were remitted, Jews were exempted from military service, Roman troops were withdrawn from Judea, religious freedom was reconfirmed, and a seaport (Joppa) and other territory in Galilee, and the coastal plain were added to Jewish control. Finally, permission was granted to rebuild the walls of Jerusalem.

Caesar also recognized that Hyrcanus II was merely a figurehead for the real authority of Antipater. He finally brought that fact into the open by appointing Antipater as procurator of Judea. Antipater was also made a Roman citizen, which was quite an honor. By that honor, Caesar acknowledged that Antipater was a friend of Rome as well as a friend of Rome's emperor. Having freed Judea of taxes due to Rome, he granted Antipater the right to tax Judea on his own.

The accomplishments of Antipater had brought signal benefits to Judea. However, he was deeply hated by the Jews, particularly the Sadducees. The outward reason for this was that he was an Idumean, a forced convert, and a descendant of the hereditary enemies of the Jews, the Edomites. However, his mother was a Jew and by law this should have made Antipater a Jew without question. Part of the hatred probably rested in his support of Hyrcanus II, who was in turn supported by the Pharisees. Yet many of the Pharisees also hated Antipater. This was probably due to the fact that with his appointment as procurator, his own power and political ambitions were out in the open.

Shortly thereafter, Caesar was murdered (44 BC). This led to a civil war in Rome. Antipater used this confusion as an opportunity to appoint his two sons to power (ca. 44 BC). He named Phasael, his oldest son, as governor of Judea. Herod, Antipater's second son, was named governor of Galilee. These appointments strengthened his own position, but increased the hatred of the Jewish leaders. As the Roman civil war dragged on, Cassius came to Syria. As we have seen, he sought to raise major funds to support his cause. Antipater complied, exacting and paying seven hundred talents. This further increased Jewish hatred. Late in 43 BC, a man named Malichos, wishing to replace Antipater, had him poisoned. Herod, in turn, avenged his father by having Malichos stabbed to death.

Phasael and Herod, Governors (ca. 44-40 BC)

Phasael's appointment as governor of Judea by Antipater, though disliked by the Jews, was accepted with relative peace. Not so was Herod's appointment in Galilee. Galilee was a hotbed of nationalism. Herod was challenged by Hezekiah, most likely a Zealot. Herod quickly sought out the insurrectionist, captured him and many of his followers, and had them all executed. For this, he was praised by the Roman governor of Syria and called to face a trial before the Sanhedrin in Jerusalem. Herod arrived in Jerusalem supported by a military guard and dressed in royal purple. He obviously intended to threaten or intimidate the Sanhedrin. In this he failed. Just before the Sanhedrin was about to convict him with a death penalty, Hyrcanus II dissolved the court, probably having been warned by Rome to do so. However, his near conviction so angered Herod that he planned to attack Jerusalem and only desisted when urged to do so both by Antipater and Phasael. They recognized that a Jewish civil war would undermine all which Antipater had accomplished. During the time of crisis, Herod's authority was significantly strengthened when the Roman governor of Syria added Samaria and Coele-Syria to his territory, making him one of the more powerful governors in the region.

In the time following the death of Antipater, which had been quickly avenged by Herod, the Roman world continued to be rocked by the consequences of Caesar's assassination. However, the defeat of Brutus and Cassius at Philippi in 42 BC brought matters to a restless peace. In 41 BC, a Jewish delegation went to Mark Antony to request removal of Phasael and Herod. Herod, however, made a direct appeal to Antony and so impressed him that both Phasael and Herod were nominated as tetrarchs by the Roman leader. This situation, however, was not to last long.

Antony's dalliance with Cleopatra of Egypt took his attention away from his responsibilities in the eastern end of the empire. The Parthians briefly invaded Syria, replacing Roman governors. At this point, Antigonus, a son of Aristobulus II, offered the Parthians his aid if they would in turn place him on the throne of Judea. The invasion succeeded for a while. Phasael and Hyrcanus II were captured, and Herod fled to Rome. Phasael committed suicide. Hyrcanus had his ears cut off, and this deformity prevented him from serving as high priest (Lev. 21:17-21). One report says that Antigonus bit off Hyrcanus's ears. Whether or not this is true, it at least reflects the Jewish opinion of their crude new ruler.

Antigonus (40-37 BC)

Antigonus was installed as king and high priest of Judea and Galilee by the Parthians. He was strictly their vassal and puppet. It was a situation which could not long endure, for Rome could not ignore it. In 39 BC, Herod, with Roman forces, invaded and made some headway, capturing both Joppa and Masada, but was unable to overrun Jerusalem. However, the Parthians' defeat by Rome in 38 BC marked the death knell of Antigonus's rule. Herod managed late in that year to seize all of Palestine with the exception of Jerusalem. Only a harsh winter prevented that. Early in 37 BC, Herod seized Jerusalem and a horrible bloodbath followed. Antigonus was taken to Antioch where he was beheaded on the orders of Antony, based upon the wishes of Herod.

The Reign of Herod (37-4 BC)

Herod Named King

At the time of the Parthian invasion of Judea, when Antigonus had captured both Phasael and Hyrcanus II, Herod had escaped to Rome. He had first fled to Idumea, his homeland, where he had secured both his family and his treasures in the safety of Masada. Turning to the Nabataens for help, he was refused either aid or sanctuary. He then fled to Egypt, where Cleopatra apparently aided him on his way to Rome. Arriving in Rome, he reported on the situation in Judea. The Romans immediately recognized the need for a strong hand to restore the situation. Antony in turn presented Herod to Octavian, who was impressed by the young man. He also remembered the aid which Herod's father had rendered to the empire. The two rulers recommended Herod to the senate and in December 40 BC he was elected king of the Jews.

At that time in Rome, those designated as kings were clearly vassals of the Roman Empire. Normally, no son could follow his father without a specific investigation. The vassal king could make no treaties and could not enter into a war on his own. He was also obligated to send troops to Rome when it was at war. He could maintain a small army for the purposes of keeping the peace. A vassal could mint coins and levy taxes.

Finally, he had the absolute power of life and death over his subjects. All these rights were granted to Herod when he was made king of the Jews.

Upon Herod's election as king of the Jews, he joined in the sacrifices to Jupiter Capitolinus in Rome. That act left no question about his religious convictions as a Jew. For him, religion appears to have been nothing more than a convenient tool to use in any way necessary to maintain power.

Herod's election as king of Judea left him in the situation of being a king without a country. Antigonus was king and high priest in Jerusalem, serving as a Parthian vassal. However, the Romans made an assault on the Parthians, who were driven from the province of Syria; Antigonus's days were numbered. Herod had made a mildly successful invasion in 39 BC. In 38 BC, accompanied by Roman forces, he began the assault which would place him upon the throne. Early in 37 BC, Herod captured Jerusalem in a bloody victory. Antigonus was carried to Antioch and beheaded. At that point, Herod began a reign which was to last more than thirty years.

Jewish Hatred

The hatred of the Jews for Herod was almost unbounded. First, they despised him for being an Idumean. Considered to be both a half-Jew and a descendent of the hated Edomites, he had little chance of ever winning their favor. Second, he had seized the throne by the overthrow of one of the Hasmoneans. It is useless to point out that these rulers themselves had been hated by the time Judea came under Roman domination. The Romans were foreigners, and the Hasmoneans were Jews. Further, the years that had passed since the end of that dynasty had dimmed the memory of its abuses. Third, Herod knew that he could only maintain himself on the throne by intimidation, fear, and oppression. When he became king, therefore, he executed forty-five leaders from among those who had supported Antigonus. These were probably primarily Sadducees. That cruel act bred hostility among all parties in Jerusalem. Fourth, Herod needed the friendship of Rome to maintain himself in power. That cost money. He despoiled many of the wealthy in Jerusalem and sent large gifts to Antony and those about him. (This may have been promised to Antony in return for the nomination to the kingship. Whether that is true, Herod certainly had to help support Antony's cause.) Clearly, Herod's relationship with his subjects was untenable from the start.

Benefits to Judea

Herod's relationships with the people of Judea were doomed from the beginning. Herod was a man of action. He never pondered what might have been but sought to do the best with what was. He began, fruitlessly it turned out, to try to win the favor of his people. He first sought to restore order. During the chaos which had come to the land, it had been overrun by bandits, brigands from the wilderness preying on the people of the land. Life was exceedingly dangerous, even in the cities. Herod quickly moved against these outlaws. He accomplished what Saul had not been able to do with David and what Antiochus Epiphanes had not been able to do with the Maccabees. He successfully pursued the outlaws to their lairs in the wilderness caves. Quickly they were either exterminated like vermin or forced to flee to other lands in order to practice their banditry. When Herod was through, Judea was probably safer than it had ever been in its history. (By the time of Jesus, however, long after the death of Herod, outlaws were again on the prowl. So much so that the parable of the good Samaritan rang true to the ears of Jesus' hearers.)

Herod also sought to win the favor of his people by at first showing favor to the remaining Hasmoneans. Upon his accession he immediately negotiated with the Parthians (such negotiations were outside the authority granted him by the Roman senate) for the release of Hyrcanus II, hoping to please the loyalists. For a number of years, Hyrcanus lived in peace and honor at Herod's court. Herod also sought to establish a legitimacy to his reign by marrying Mariamne, a Hasmonean princess. She was the grandaughter of Aristobulus II through her father and of Hyrcanus II through her mother. In doing this, he had to divorce his first wife, Doris. The marriage with Mariamne was not merely one of expediency, however; Herod seems to have loved her passionately.

An additional attempt to win popular support was Herod's bestowing of major honors upon two leaders of the Pharisees, Abtalion and Shemaiah. This was quite significant, in that the Pharisees influenced more people in Judea than any of the other parties. He also carefully refused, in respect of Jewish law, to have any images inscribed on his coins. Further, he avoided, at least until late in his reign when all this was seen to have been hopeless, bringing any images into Jerusalem.

Legally, from a Roman standpoint, Herod could have acted as high priest. Knowing what that would do to any hopes of support, he appointed a high priest from among the Babylonian Jews by the name of Hananel. This was done to avoid offending any party in Jerusalem by selecting someone from some other party as high priest. However, Herod's mother-in-law felt that her son Aristobulus, being a grandson of Hyrcanus II, was the rightful heir to the office. She persuaded Herod to depose Hananel and appoint the seventeen-year-old Aristobulus. Tragically, the youthful high priest drowned shortly thereafter in a swimming accident, and Hananel was reinstated. He served as high priest from 36-30 BC. Rumors in Jerusalem charged Herod with the death of Aristobulus. His later life-style makes the rumor plausible, but no other evidence exists to support the charge.

The Aristobulus crisis had international implications for Herod. Cleopatra, in her dalliances with Mark Antony, had ambitions to rule over Judea as a former part of the Ptolemaic empire. Alexandra, the mother of Aristobulus, had apparently been in communication with Cleopatra, suggesting that the Egyptian queen appoint her son as king. Each woman had planned on ruling through the boy-king. Cleopatra used her influence on Antony to get him to investigate the charges against Herod. Thus Herod was summoned to Laodicea in Syria, where he was acquitted of the charges. Rumor had it that Herod bribed Antony. On the other hand, Antony sent word to Cleopatra, saying, "One must not investigate too closely the official acts of a king, lest he ceases to be really a king" (Josephus, *Antiquities*, XV, 76).

Building Projects

Herod also sought to win the favor of the people by massive building projects. Samaria was rebuilt with the new name of Sebaste, in honor of Augustus. (*Sebaste* is the Greek word for Augustus). He also erected a completely new port, calling it Caesarea, and rebuilt ancient Aphek, calling it Antipatris. At Jericho, Herod built a magnificent winter palace with gardens and swimming pools. Twelve to fifteen major cities were built or rebuilt during his reign. In addition, numerous new fortresses were built on the borders of Judea or on the major approaches to Jerusalem. Among these were Masada in the wilderness of En-gedi and Machaerus in the extreme south of Perea.

In Jerusalem, Herod entered into major building projects as well. His own palace dominated the city. Further, he built the fortress of Antonia to the northwest of the Temple area. Perhaps his most significant project was rebuilding the Temple itself. This was begun about 20-19 BC. It was still in process during the lifetime of Jesus and was not completed until AD 64. It was planned as a magnificent center of worship and designed to appeal to and to appease the orthodox Pharisees as well as the Sadducees. No destruction of the old Temple was begun until supplies to start the new one were already on the site. The new building was twice the size as the old one. Further, in planning the building, only priests were used in those areas too sacred for nonpriests to enter.

With all of this, Herod failed to win the support of his people. Despite the glory and honor he brought to them, despite his catering to their religious sensibilities, and despite the bringing of peace and prosperity to the land, he was still not accepted. Even despite his use of his own wealth to purchase and distribute grain in a time of famine, he was generally a hated figure. This being so, in the latter days of his reign, he gave up all attempts to win friends among a hostile populace.

International Relations

During Herod's early years as king of Judea, the international situation was anything but settled. He sought to follow the same policy which had served his father, Antipater, so well. He was absolutely loyal to Rome and wholeheartedly supported whichever Roman figure was in control of Palestine.

During the early days of Herod's rule, the conflict between Antony and Octavian grew sharply, primarily due to Antony's marriage with Cleopatra in 36 BC. In the meantime, Cleopatra coveted the territories of Palestine which had been a part of the Ptolemaic empire in the third century BC. While Antony did not give her Judea, he did give her some territory near Jericho for which Herod paid her an annual rent of two hundred talents. Antony also gave her some Transjordan territory near the Sea of Galilee which was controlled by the Nabateans and from which she was to receive an equal rent.

However, Cleopatra's ambition may also have inadvertently saved the kingship for Herod. In 32 BC, the Nabateans failed to pay their annual tribute to the queen of Egypt. She, in turn, sought Herod's aid in getting it. Recognizing the relationship between Cleopatra and Antony, Herod set forth on a military expedition against the Nabateans. He was involved in this when Antony gathered his forces for what was to be the final conflict with Octavian. This meant that Herod was not present at the Battle of Actium where Antony was finally overthrown.

Octavian went to Rhodes following Actium. There Herod was summoned (along with others) to deal with the master of the Roman Empire. Openly admitting his unswerving allegiance to Antony (how could he have denied it?), he also claimed the same allegiance to Rome. Herod then persuaded Octavian that he would give the new ruler the same loyalty and support. Octavian believed him and confirmed him in his position. He also gave back to Herod the region Antony had given Cleopatra, along with several additional territories. This was the beginning of a long and profitable relationship between Octavian and Herod. The relationship was clearly profitable to both men, but it was also profitable to Judea and her people.

In 20 BC, and again in 12 BC, Augustus (as he was called after 27 BC) gave additional territories to Herod. The ruler of the Jews was also given some authority over all of Syria. Herod, on the other hand, made at least two trips to Rome and on several occasions sent troops to participate in Roman military activities. Many of his building projects were for the purpose of honoring the Roman emperor. He did institute an oath of loyalty to Rome and to Augustus late in his reign which created a problem with the Pharisees and the Essenes.

The only apparent problem which Herod had with Augustus was in 27 BC. At that time, Herod had sought to eliminate some Arab bandits in the region of Trachonitis which Octavian had given him. When this was reported to the emperor, he felt that Herod had violated the terms of his kingship, having gone to war without Roman permission. Herod sent his friend and court chronicler to plead his case before Octavian, convincing him that Herod had sought to deal effectively with problems which required immediate attention and that neither disobedience nor disloyalty had been involved.

Herod's Family

Herod's family life was the source of most of his problems. The king of Judea was a very jealous man, and his jealousy frequently moved him to instability, if not outright insanity. This jealousy was not aided by the intrigues of his mother-in-law, Alexandra, nor by the Hasmonean loyalties of his wife, Mariamne.

The whole sordid story of Herod's domestic troubles are told in detail in Josephus. It is sufficient here simply to summarize them. They began with the swimming death of the young high priest, Aristobulus. This clearly alienated his mother-in-law and perhaps began the alienation of his wife.

When, as a consequence of that event, Herod was called to report to Antony, he left his government in the hands of Joseph, who was both his uncle and his brother-in-law, being married to Herod's sister Salome. Joseph was instructed if Herod were executed by Antony to immediately put Mariamne to death. So jealous was Herod that he would not allow any other man to have his wife.

Perhaps instigated by his wife, Salome (who was also jealous of Mariamne), Joseph revealed Herod's orders to Mariamne. He apparently thought by this to convince her of the depth of Herod's love. Suffice it to say, Mariamne was not particularly impressed. Upon Herod's return, she confronted him with his cruel order. From that time her love and devotion cooled perceptibly and steadily.

Herod assumed that Joseph would not have revealed his secret orders if he had not been involved with Mariamne in adultery. This suspicion was undergirded when Salome openly accused him of such. Herod, therefore, had Joseph executed without a trial.

Due to his ongoing fear of the family of the Hasmoneans, Herod had Hyrcanus II executed, accusing him of attempting to gain Nabatean support to overthrow Herod (ca. 30 BC). Salome accused Mariamne of adultery again, this time with one Sohemus whom Herod had left in charge when he went to meet Octavian after the death of Antony. Sohemus was also executed without a trial. In addition, Mariamne was tried, condemned, and executed about 29 BC. His grief over her death made Herod deeply ill.

In 28 BC, during Herod's illness and intense depression, Alexandra, Mariamne's mother, was charged with trying to seize power for the Hasmoneans. In response, Herod had her executed.

Things settled down in his family for a while, but after some twelve to fifteen years, troubles began between Herod and three of his sons. Herod had a son by Doris (his first wife) named Antipater and two sons by Mariamne named Alexander and Aristobulus. Because of Herod's putting away of Doris for Mariamne and because of his execution of Mariamne, the relationship between these half-brothers was anything but cordial, if not openly hostile. Herod began to suspect, based on the charges of Antipater and Salome, that Alexander and Aristobulus were planning to avenge their mother's death. They all made a trip to Rome where Augustus effected a temporary reconciliation in 12 BC.

However the charges continued, and they were apparently not without some substance. Herod sent his evidence to Augustus for a judgment. As Herod's sons, Alexander and Aristobulus were Roman citizens and could not be executed without the permission of the emperor. Augustus read the evidence and gave Herod permission to carry out any judgment which a court might render. A trial was held, the sons were convicted, and they were executed by strangulation at Sebaste in 7 BC. At that time,

Herod became aware of how deep the support for his sons was among the army groups. He, therefore, had about three hundred army officers put to death because of the supposed (real?) threat of rebellion.

Shortly thereafter, Antipater, who at one time had been designated to be Herod's successor, came under suspicion. He, too, was tried and convicted. Augustus again approved the sentence, and he was executed in 4 BC., shortly before Herod's death. This whole episode brought forth Augustus's famous pun: "It is better to be Herod's pig (*huis,* which as a Jew he would not kill) than Herod's son (*huios*)."

It goes without saying that Herod was both tragically insecure and insanely jealous. It is also apparent that he was violent and oppressive. Such a character could easily have ordered the slaughter of the infants of Bethlehem; the act would have been quite characteristic. On the other hand, we must also admit that Herod was not blessed by a loyal, undergirding family. Their actions were, at the least, unsupportive. They were generally cruel and avaricious in their relations with one another and with Herod. He had to be strong and decisive in order to maintain his control for so long. Perhaps it is a mark of his ability that he survived to die a natural death.

Herod's Last Days

It was obvious, at least from 5 BC, that Herod was a dying man. The actual nature of his illness is unknown and undiagnosable from the descriptions which we have of it. Probably it was some form of cancer, but that is by no means certain. All Judea knew of his approaching death, and most people looked forward to it.

During Herod's last days an event occurred, unmentioned in other historical records outside the New Testament, which was to shake the world. Jesus was born in Bethlehem of Judea. When Parthian Magi came to Jerusalem seeking the king of the Jews, Herod's ever-present jealousy was aroused. Being told by his own counselors of the prophecy of Bethlehem as the birthplace, Herod directed the Magi there. When he was later unable to find the specific child, he had every male child under the age of two executed. Bethlehem being a small town, that would have been no great number. The entire act, however, is quite characteristic of this violent, dying man.

In the earlier part of his reign, Herod had sought to keep the letter of the law in a vain attempt to win the support of some of the people, including the Pharisees. By the end of his reign he had given up that futile hope. Toward his death he had allowed the imprinting of an eagle (the symbol of Rome, perhaps) upon his coins. The height of his folly is seen, however, by his hanging a gilded eagle over the gate of the Temple. This coupled with Herod's approaching death led two rabbis, Judas and Matthias, leaders of the Pharisees, to urge upon their disciples the merit of destroying such an abhorrent image. When premature news of Herod's death came from Jericho, the disciples went forth and tore the image down. However, Herod was not dead. In retaliation, Herod had the two rabbis and a number of their disciples burned at the stake. This was March 11, 4 BC. On the next night, March 12, there was an eclipse of the moon. The Pharisees and many of the people of Jerusalem saw in this a symbol of the divine horror at the martydom of Judas and Mathias.

Five days before Herod's death, Augustus approved the execution of Antipater, and it was quickly carried out. As his death approached, Herod was intensely aware of the deep hatred which his people held for him. He could not bear to think of the rejoicing which would accompany his death. To avoid this, he made his sister Salome promise that a large group of Jewish leaders who had been brought to his palace at Jericho would be executed immediately after his death. That was to ensure mourning throughout the land. Fortunately, that was a promise Salome did not keep.

Shortly thereafter Herod died. Salome and Archelaus, Herod's son and chief beneficiary, conducted the funeral. Beginning in the amphitheater in Jericho, the funeral procession carried his body with pomp and ceremony to the Herodium south of Jerusalem. There he was buried as he had lived, in ostentatious luxury. Riots throughout Judea were dealt with summarily by Archelaus. About three thousand Jews perished in the fighting. As Herod wished, great mourning accompanied his death, but not in the manner he had intended.

Summation

Herod became known as Herod the Great. This title is more to distinguish him from other members of his family with the same name than it is to evaluate him. On the other hand, if greatness is measured in terms of length of reign, building, territorial expansion, or political expertise, he truly deserves the title. However, in terms of the love, loyalty, or respect of subjects or family, no one has less deserved the title of "the Great." He left a legacy of violence and hostility. These were soon to produce their harvest of bitter fruit for Judea.

Herod was a man of mixed character. Outside of Judea proper, he was an active Hellenist. Inside, he was a loyal Jew. Capable of intense love and loyalty, he was also capable of hatred and bitter cruelty. More than anything else, Herod loved Herod.

The Consequences of the Early Roman Rule

As we have seen, the period of the early Roman domination of Judea falls into two major divisions. The first three decades were turbulent, primarily because the entire Roman empire was turbulent and stormy during that era. The turbulence began to settle down with the accession of Herod as king of Judea in 37 BC and fully settled with the rise of Octavian to the sole rulership of the region in 31 BC. In surveying the almost sixty years which stretch from Pompey's capture of the Temple to the death of Herod, several developments appear to be worth noting.

The Zealots

The Zealots are first mentioned during the reign of Herod. Their prime concern rested in the belief that God alone was king over the Jews. Because of that belief, they would not rest until every foreign soldier and every semblance of foreign authority was swept from the land. Two basic strands appear to have fed into this party of the Jews. They originated as a distinct party in Galilee, probably arising from the nationalism that springs from new commitments. Under the Hasmoneans (see the preceding chapter), Galilee had been brought back into mainstream Judaism. Because of this, their regional commitment was more to the nation than the Torah. Their origins in Galilee may also go deep in the grinding poverty which was experienced there. When abject poverty makes life untenable, anything, even death, becomes preferable. To throw off the Roman yoke might not help, but to their minds the attempt could not make matters any worse.

The second major root of the Zealot party can be found among the Pharisees in Judea. They, too, perceived of God as King. Any attempt to make them disobey the Torah or the command of their Divine King was to be eliminated. Of this nature was the belief which led them to the violent destruction of the Temple eagle in the last days of Herod. However, in the last analysis, their commitment was to the Torah and not to the nation. Thus it was that finally most Pharisees disassociated themselves from the Zealot ties.

The Herodians

As a party, the Herodians are mentioned only in the New Testament (Matt. 22:16; Mark 3:6; 12:13). Josephus did speak of a group known as "followers of Herod" without actually calling them Herodians. We know nothing about them other than what can be surmised. They were apparently supporters of Herod's aims. This most likely means that they saw Judea's only hope as being loyal and obedient servants of Rome. Such a belief would put them in direct and unavoidable opposition to the Zealots, as well as to the Pharisees.

Sadducees and Pharisees

No mention of the Sadducees occurs in references from this period. This is probably due to the drastic reduction in their numbers and influence during Pompey's campaign, in the early rebellions of this era, and in Herod's drastic measures taken toward the supporters of Antigonus. The fall of the Hasmoneans had to take a major toll on this group. Some obviously survived, for they do show up again in the New Testament era.

On the other hand, the Pharisees were visibly present and quite vocal during this time. Herod had several direct confrontations with them. From the beginning of his reign, he sought their support. Failing to achieve this, he confronted them as enemies, putting some of them to death. He excused them from taking an oath of allegiance to him, but sought to force them to pledge allegiance to Rome and Augustus. In this he failed. They were utterly loyal to their God and His Torah. On the other hand, they accepted the rule of Rome as a just punishment for the nation's disobedience to the Law. Wielding major influence upon the people, they are said to have numbered only about six thousand actual adherents during the early days of Herod. They probably never numbered more than ten thousand.

Qumran and the Essenes

While there is still debate as to whether the people of Qumran and the Essenes are to be identified, the best evidence appears to show a genuine relationship. Herod is said to have treated the Essenes with tolerance, as one of them reportedly told him as a boy that he would one day be king of the Jews. From the latter days of the Hasmoneans, they had reacted with utter disapproval toward their priest-kings. Having withdrawn to the desert and established their enclave at Qumran, their leader, "The Teacher of Righteousness," had led them to believe that they were in the last days. They placed a major emphasis upon the prophets rather than upon the Torah. However, they were deeply concerned with the practical living out of the Torah. Perhaps because of his boyhood experience or perhaps because of their utter pacifism, Herod exempted them from an oath of loyalty either to Rome or to Augustus.

Peace and Prosperity

The early days of the Roman era brought neither peace nor prosperity. However, by 31 BC, peace settled down over the region. As we have seen, peace under Herod was no gentle thing, but was harsh and cruel for those who opposed either him or Rome. By and large, however, this did not affect most of the people. Almost thirty years without a major conflict was more than the region had experienced since the coming of Alexander the Great.

Prosperity was a different matter. Herod's major building projects furnished massive employment for the people of Judea. In Galilee, poverty was the rule of the day. Excavations in Jerusalem show significant wealth. However, the rural population there also probably experienced some of the poverty of Galilee. Herod's projects required large amounts of taxes. These were probably gathered through the old Ptolemaic system of tax farmers. In general they were Jews who bought the right to collect taxes. In so doing, they came to be considered traitors by their own people and became outcasts from Jewish society. The government, however, depended upon them.

Rome and Messianism

Herod would have viewed as his greatest failure his inability to win, if not love, at least respect and admiration. He would have viewed as his second greatest failure his inability to get his people to recognize that Rome was there to stay. As far as he was concerned, Judea's only hope for survival rested in living peacefully within the Roman Empire. Future events showed him to be absolutely correct.

However, Herod's dream was not to be. The more he sought to lead his people in being a full part of the empire, the more they resisted. As a part of that resistance, the Zealots arose. Out of the rise of the Zealots came the rise of a renewed messianism. Looking for and longing for the absolute deliverance from foreign rule, these people began to reinterpret the Old Testament teachings relating to the coming of God's messiah. This showed up in differing ways among the groups within Judea extending from the militant Zealots on one hand to the pacifists of Qumran on the other. This hope led individual leaders among the Zealots to call themselves "messiah" and to seek to gather followers in order to drive

Rome from Judean soil. That, too, was to have bitter fruit in the not-too-distant future.

Herod had presided over a time of peace for his people. But the seed sown then were to provide anything but peace among his successors. The Roman rule continued, but it brought with it a new turbulence for Judea.

8

The New Testament Era
(4 BC-AD 66)

In one sense the interbiblical period technically ended with the birth of Jesus, for there the New Testament begins. For Judaism, as well as for early Christianity, this era went on until the end of the Second Jewish Revolt, when the nation actually ceased to exist. For that reason, I am including this chapter and the one following. This is not intended in any way to be a history of the New Testament or a life of Jesus or Paul. I am primarily concerned here with what happened to the Jews, the people of the Old Testament, in this era. Only where their story intersects Christian history will I deal with the New Testament.

The events of the period following the death of Herod (4 BC) and the beginning of the First Jewish Revolt (AD 66) are confusing. They are confusing chronologically and geographically. They were confusing as they were lived out. Without adequate sources for correlation and evaluation, the historian is left to make the best use of the sources and, at the same time, must regularly hang question marks over conclusions. The Roman administrative regions changed with changes in politics. Borders were uncertain much of the time. However, enough can be discerned to give us a relatively good general picture, even if the details must at times be hazy.

For the Jewish people of Palestine, it was a difficult time. In this seventy-year period, Judea was ruled by an ethnarch, seven procurators, a king, and seven more procurators. Many of these leaders were brutal, some were venal, and almost all were incompetent. The Jewish people seldom experienced the best Rome had to offer. As a consequence, Rome never saw the best of the Jewish people. They were seen as violent, reactionary, revolutionary, disloyal, and obstinate. But we can only deal with history as it was. The discussion of what might have been, while fascinating, is but a passing shadow when seen against what was. What was isn't pretty, but it must be seen and an attempt must be made to understand it.

Chronological Table
The New Testament Era (4 BC-AD 66)

Rome	Judea and Samaria	Galilee and Perea	Northern Transjordan
Augustus (27 BC-AD 14)	Archelaus, Ethnarch (4 BC-AD 6)	Herod Antipas Tetrarch (4 BC-AD 39)	Philip, Tetrarch (4 BC-AD 34)
	Procurators: Coponius (6-9) Ambibulus (9-12)		
Tiberius (14-37)	Rufus (12-15) Valerius Gratus (15-26)		
Sejanus executed (31)	Pontius Pilate (26-36) Marcellus (36)		Syrian Rule (34-37)
Caligula (37-41)	Marullus (37-41)		Agrippa I, King (37-44)
Claudius (41-54)	Agrippa I, King (41-46)	Agrippa, I, King (40-44)	
	Procurators: Cuspius Fadus (44-46) Theudas emerges (45) Tiberius Alexander (46-48) Famine (ca. 46) Ventidus Cumanus (48-52)		Agrippa II(49-92/93) King of Chalcis (49)
	Felix (52-60)		Philip's tetrarchy added (53) Galilee and Perea added (54/55)

Nero (54-68)   Paul arrested (ca. 58)
   Rome burns Festus (60-62)
     (64)   Albinus (62-64)
             Florus (64-66)

Developments in Rome

Augustus (27 BC-AD 14)

At the death of Herod, Augustus was still emperor of Rome; he ruled from 27 BC to AD 14. During Herod's final years, the emperor had been less than enthusiastic about Herod and the developments in Palestine. It must be remembered that Herod ruled as king only by permission of the emperor. Herod had established in his will which of his sons should succeed him and over what territories they would rule. These provisions, however, were of no effect unless Augustus approved. A deputation from Jerusalem tried to get Augustus to deny Herod's last wishes and to reestablish Judea with the Temple as its religious center and a Roman governor performing the civil duties. Under the urging of Nicolas of Damascus (court historian of Herod and friend of Augustus), Herod's will was approved. Archelaus was appointed ethnarch of Judea and Samaria, Philip was made tetrarch (slightly lower) of the region northeast of Galilee, and Antipas was made tetrarch of Galilee and Perea (southern Transjordan).

Archelaus's rule was so atrocious that a combined delegation of Judeans and Samaritans pleaded with Augustus for his removal. Augustus was loyal to his servants, but his prime concern was peace in the empire. Thus, Archelaus was recalled in AD 6 and banished to the Rhone Valley. Judea, along with Samaria, was made into a third-class province, to be ruled over by a procurator appointed by the emperor.

Throughout this period, the terms *procurator* and *prefect,* while technically different, seem to have been used interchangeably. Procurators were generally chosen from the second level of Roman society, the equestrians. Not wishing to run the risk of such minor figures attempting to establish themselves too firmly or being too tempted to corruption, Augustus appointed these men for terms of three years only.

With the change in the status of the region of Judea, it was important that a proper assessment for the purpose of taxation be made. Thus a census was carried out by Quirinus, the legate of Syria in AD 6.

Tiberius (AD 14-37)

Augustus died in AD 14 and was succeeded by Tiberius (AD 14-37), his adopted son, the child of his wife Livia by her first husband. Tiberius showed himself to be an able ruler. He was very concerned with the conditions under which his subjects lived, even in the remotest regions of the empire. Thus he lived and ran the empire in a relatively austere style, generally being able therefore to reduce taxes. He worked for stability in government and made his appointments for considerably longer periods of service than Augustus had done.

Tiberius, unfortunately, was unpopular with the Roman senate, and this led to unrest at the center of the empire. He entrusted much of the operation of the empire to the prefect of his imperial guard, Sejanus. Sejanus brought many charges of treason to Tiberius, preying on the emperor's suspicions. It became quite important in the latter part of Tiberius's reign to be identified as a "Friend of Caesar." This may have been behind the threat issued by the leaders of Jerusalem to Pilate that if he released Jesus, he would not be "Caesar's friend" *(amicus Caesaris)*. Tiberius's fear of treachery finally reached even to Sejanus himself, who was executed for treason in AD 31. Tiberius, with the encouragement of Sejanus, had moved to the Island of Capri in AD 26 from which he ruled by correspondence. Pilate was appointed in AD 26, so he was clearly a protege of Sejanus. Sejanus's execution, therefore, must have thrust fear into Pilate's heart. Tiberius's last six years are quite obscure. He died in AD 37.

Caligula (AD 37-41)

Tiberius was succeeded by the grandson of Germanicus, one of Rome's leading generals. He was Tiberius's nephew, had been his rival, and became his heir. Numerous deaths (executions, assassinations, etc.) in the family, thus, let the empire fall on the shoulders of Caius, nick-named Caligula. He had grown up as a military child with his father's troops. As a three- and four-year old, he had constantly worn the military-style boots of the soldiers. They had lovingly called him *Caligula,* "Little Boots." His father had died in AD 19, perhaps by poison, when Caius was only seven. His mother was arrested when he was seventeen. He lived in turn with two elderly matriarchs, both of whom died before he became emperor in AD 37. All of this was enough to distort his thinking.

Shortly after he became emperor, Caligula became desperately ill (AD

38). Though he recovered to some degree, he was left with a severe mental disorder. How much of his mental problems was due to his illness and how much to his upbringing we do not know. As a result, however, he made the most ridiculous decisions. He had his horse made a Roman senator. He also had himself declared to be a god, to be worshiped throughout the empire. He ordered that a statue of himself be erected in the Temple of Jerusalem. We have no way of knowing what would have happened had this been done. As a consequence of his many cruelties to nobles and notables in Rome, he was assassinated in AD 41 by soldiers of the Praetorian Guard. Thus his orders concerning Jerusalem were never carried out.

Claudius (AD 41-54)

Up to this point, the Roman senate had named the emperor. However, this time the army nominated the emperor and the senate's approval, though still officially necessary, was only a rubber stamp upon a decision already made. Following the murder of Caligula, the Praetorian Guard rampaged through the imperial palace. Claudius was found hiding, in terror for his life. The guard ridiculed and mocked him and then, apparently with great irony, believing him to be someone they could control, named him emperor. They had every reason to believe they could control him, for his whole life had been characterized by a sense of failure and inferiority, coupled with introversion and bad health.

Claudius was the uncle of Caligula, a very pale shadow of the flambouyant Germanicus. His lineage gave him a tenuous but legitimate claim upon the throne. The senate was full of opposition to his nomination as emperor, but in fear of the army approved it. In all honesty, we must note that no one was as opposed to Claudius's nomination as he was himself. Further, we must also note that Claudius overcame both his own and others' opposition and became a significantly better-than-average emperor.

Claudius turned out to be a wise ruler and a capable administrator. For most of his appointments, he turned to the freedmen of the empire, rather than to the nobles. These were people who had served their masters so well as slaves, being business and estate managers, military aides, and the like, that they had been given freedom. They were people who knew how to use the practical art of politics in order to get things done. They knew backstairs gossip, the private weaknesses of public people, and were able to use these things to accomplish their tasks. In short, they became Claudius's and Rome's bureaucrats. Claudius further extended Roman citizenship to many who had not earlier qualified.

The emperor also turned out to be a military leader of some ability. He added several provinces to the empire, including Mauretania and Britain. The emperor personally participated in part of the Britannic campaign, obliterating his reputation for softness and incompetence.

Married four times, he had difficulties with his family. Their jealousy and struggle to succeed him caused him significant problems and sorrow. He was an unlikely candidate for greatness. However, having had greatness thrust upon him, he rose to meet its challenge and must go down as one of the abler of Rome's rulers. His death, in AD 54, left a significant vacancy in the affairs of Rome and its empire.

Nero (AD 54-68)

Claudius's fourth wife was Agrippina, a daughter of Germanicus. She brought a son by a former marriage, a great-nephew of Claudius, to the marriage. She then persuaded Claudius to adopt him and name him as his heir in AD 50. Shortly thereafter, Britannicus, Claudius' own son (and the legal heir) died, probably by poisoning (AD 55). Thus, Agrippina's son, Nero, succeeded without conflict.

At the beginning of Nero's reign, he showed himself to be a rather capable administrator. However, two other traits also showed up which dominated his later years. He wished to be an artist in many fields of endeavor. This led to a self-indulgence of the senses. He also would not put up with opposition, or even with threats of opposition. This brought forth a streak of violence for which, while not as extreme as in some other emperors, he is most remembered.

In order to throw off any threat or fear of domination by those who had helped him to power, he murdered both his mother, Agrippina, and his wife, Octavia. He began to promote all sorts of musical contests and athletic games, in which he participated. He always won. (Who would dare defeat him?) His lavish entertainments led to great financial need. To meet these needs, he began to accuse the wealthiest Roman nobles of treason. Upon their execution, the emperor confiscated their property. External wars, which he had no wish to fight, also depleted his finances.

In AD 64, a major part of Rome burned in a fire that lasted for days. Nero was suspected of setting the fire because he wished to rebuild the city to suit his own tastes. During the fire, he is said to have joyfully recited poetry to the accompaniment of a lyre in anticipation of the new city's beauty (thus the expression of Nero's fiddling while Rome burned).

The hostility of the people at the destruction of their homes and businesses was foolishly unexpected. Lest it be turned upon himself, Nero made the Christians the scapegoats. This led to an intense persecution which may have resulted in the executions of both Peter and Paul.

A plot to assassinate Nero in AD 65 failed but served to drive him even further into violent and oppressive practices. The emperor made a trip to Cenchreae to construct a canal across the Isthmus of Corinth, as well as to have a tour of games and concerts. The emperor was the one most honored by the tour. Additional executions occurred along the way, particularly of leaders who had been either too unsuccessful or too successful in the competitions.

In AD 67, Nero was urged to return to Rome to deal with its increasing unrest. His excesses had cost him friends and had strengthened enemies. The Praetorian Guard once again arose, and Nero fled for his life. A frightened and dejected emperor committed suicide in June AD 68. Though Nero wished to be known as an artistic genius, he is not so remembered in world history. His name is a synonymn for a selfish, sadistic tyrant and an insensitive, inhuman beast.

Palestine to Agrippa I (4 BC-AD 41)

Upon the death of Herod the Great (4 BC), the situation in Palestine was quite uncertain. In his last will, Herod had named three of his sons, Archelaus, Herod Antipas, and Philip, as his successors. However, as we have seen, Herod himself had served at the will of the Roman emperor, Augustus. No one could succeed Herod without Augustus's approval. Further, the very fact that Herod named three sons to divide his responsibilities shows that in his opinion, no one of them was capable of following him. History proved him right.

Even before his successors could be considered, a major rebellion broke out in Judea. Archelaus had to make two attempts before he finally brought this to a very bloody conclusion. Then he and his brothers made their journey to Rome to see Augustus. They hoped to have Herod's will ratified. Others also made the journey to Rome with different hopes. A Jewish delegation made the journey to plead with Augustus that none of Herod's family should succeed him. They sought to have the high priest reinstituted as ruler, with military authority resting in the Roman governor of Syria. A delegation representing the Greek cities of Hippus, Gadara, and Gaza presented itself to Augustus. They wanted to be excluded from any Herodian rule and to be made a direct part of the Roman province of Syria.

While Augustus was making up his mind, another revolt broke out in Judea. The Syrian governor, Varus, marched into the region and crushed the revolt. He left a legion behind to maintain the peace. When their commander, Sabinus, oppressed the Jews, a new rebellion broke out. This spread even to Perea and to Galilee. Varus quickly returned and again defeated the rebels. As an object lesson of the consequences of such rebellion, Varus crucified two thousand of the rebels. All of this shows the inherent instability of Judea and surely influenced Augustus in making his decision. Herod at least had essentially maintained peace. Augustus hoped for the same from Herod's sons. On the other hand, the Jews' desire to be rid of an Herodian king was also significant.

Augustus apparently thought he had reached a satisfactory solution with a compromise of sorts. He ratified Herod's will by assigning Judea, Samaria, and Idumea to Archelaus, giving Galilee and Perea to Herod Antipas, and yielding the northern Transjordan region (Auranitis, Trachonitis, and Ituraea) to Philip. The three petitioning Greek cities were incorporated into Syria. However, none of Herod's sons was made king. Archelaus was made ethnarch and Antipas and Philip were made tetrarchs. An ethnarch had less power and independence than a king and a tetrarch had even less than an ethnarch. The actual limits varied from time to time, but the relative relationship was always consistent.

Judea and Samaria: Archelaus (4 BC-AD 6)

Archelaus was assigned the territory of Judea, Samaria, and Idumea. Although he was only given the title of ethnarch, Augustus promised him the title of king at a later time if he should prove worthy of it. Of all Herod's sons, however, Archelaus has the worst reputation. According to Josephus, Archelaus deposed and appointed high priests at will. This created a scandal in Jerusalem. Equally as scandalous, and in some circles more so, was his marriage. His wife, Glaphyra, had first been married to his half-brother Alexander who had been executed in 7 BC. After Alexander's death she had married Juba, king of Mauretania. She was divorced by him and returned to her home. Archelaus met her there, fell in love, and divorced his wife. Since Glaphyra had children by Alexander, this new marriage was illegal under Jewish Levitical law. Even though she died soon after, the offense remained in the minds of the people.

As his father's son, Archelaus devoted himself to several major building projects. Among these was a major aqueduct to carry water to the palm groves near Jericho and Scythopolis. However, he was his father's son in other ways as well: He governed his people with a harsh hand. The statement that because of him Joseph feared to bring Mary and the young Jesus back to Bethlehem but took them to Nazareth instead is well founded according to what we know of him (cf. Matt. 2:22). In fact, so oppressive was his misgovernment that the Jews and the Samaritans united in their hatred of him. They formed a joint delegation and went to Augustus, pleading for relief.

Archelaus was summoned by Augustus to report to him on the situation in Judea. Augustus was concerned with two things: peace in the empire and the maintenance of the flow of trade and taxes. Archelaus received banishment to the Rhone Valley in Gaul from the hand of the emperor. He was fortunate not to have been executed by Augustus. Greater men than he had been executed for lesser difficulties. He could probably credit his survival to the respect which Augustus had for his father, Herod.

Judea and Samaria: The Early Procurators (AD 6-41)

With the deposition of Archelaus, Augustus reorganized that part of his empire, placing Judea, Samaria, and Idumea directly under Roman control and making them politically part of the province of Syria. Technically they were directly ruled by a procurator who was responsible to the governor of Syria. In actual fact, they were relatively independent in matters of government and military activity. The official residence for the procurators was established in Caesarea. They took up residence in Jerusalem only during times of specific or imminent danger. This explains why they moved into Jerusalem at the times of the great feasts. That is why Pilate was in Jerusalem at the Passover when Jesus was crucified.

The first procurator of Judea was Coponius (AD 6-9). He was the personal agent of the emperor but was subordinate to the governor of Syria. The transition to a Roman province demanded that a census be taken to register property and to count people for the purposes of taxation. Quirinius, the legate of Syria was assigned this task in AD 6.

The taking of the census aroused intense opposition among the Jews. The issue of foreign taxation was sensitive enough. However, they believed that taking a census was an offense against God (cf. 2 Sam. 24). Joazar, the high priest at the time who had been appointed by Quirinius, sought to appease the people and led most of them to accept the census. However, a minority, led by Judas of Galilee, openly rebelled. This is probably the same Judas who was involved in a revolt at the time of

Herod's death (4 BC). This new rebellion was put down quickly and with severity. Judas apparently lost his life in the fighting. That episode is mentioned in the speech of Gamaliel in reference to a revolt in the days of the enrollment (Acts 5:37). Although the revolt was crushed, its ideals became a part of the movement of the Zealots. It simmered under the surface until it flamed forth again in AD 66. Although Joazar supported the policy of Quirinius, he was for some reason subsequently deposed by Quirinius. Annas was then appointed high priest. This is the same Annas who is mentioned in the New Testament and whose son-in-law Caiaphas was high priest in the time of Jesus.

With the advent of the period of the procurators, two major differences showed up in the administration of the territory of Judea. First, the procurators had the authority to impose the death penalty. Roman citizens still could appeal the sentence of the governor to the emperor. Second, the Roman procurators tried to be sensitive to the beliefs of the Jews, but they frequently acted out of ignorance. They created problems which were always ready to flash into open rebellion. On occasion, the emperors specifically ordered their procurators to exercise sensitivity to the Jews' beliefs.

Following Coponius, the next two procurators were also appointed by Augustus. Other than their names, Ambibulus (AD 9-12) and Rufus (AD 12-15), we know nothing of them. Then Tiberius came to the throne in AD 14. In AD 15, he appointed his first Judean procurator, Valerius Gratus (AD 15-26). With that appointment, the procedure of short appointments was altered in an attempt to achieve some degree of stability. Valerius Gratus must have significantly increased taxes, for in AD 17 an appeal was made to Tiberius for relief. Nothing is known of his decision. However, in the light of his policy of reducing taxes and since no other complaint was lodged, we can probably assume that the burden was eased significantly. Valerius Gratus also appointed four high priests during his term of service. Annas was deposed in favor of the appointment of Ishmael. Ishmael was deposed, and Annas's son Eleazar was appointed. In turn, Eleazar was deposed, and Simon was appointed. Finally, he, too, was deposed, and Caiaphas, the son-in-law of Annas, was appointed. The frequency of such appointments, when they became effective upon the deposition of others rather than upon death, probably indicates that Valerius was taking bribes for appointments.

After Valerius, Pontius Pilate was appointed to serve as the procurator of Judea. He served from AD 26 to 36. Pontius Pilate lives in history because he had the misfortune of being procurator in Judea during the time of Jesus, and it was his edict which eventually put Him to death. In that trial, Pilate is not portrayed as an enemy of the Jews. He is seen as a stubborn man, eager to add insult to those over whom he ruled. His decision to keep the inscription, "King of the Jews," reveals these traits in him.

Josephus recorded that Pilate was utterly despised by the Jews. Two events show why. Early in Pilate's rule, he brought the shields of his troops into Jerusalem. Since they bore the image of the emperor, this was an outrage against Jewish sensibilities. As this was in direct disobedience of an imperial order, Pilate probably did it with the support of some outside authority. It is possible that this was done at the instigation of Sejanus, the prefect of the imperial guard who was accused of having been anti-Semitic. The reaction of the Jews was so quick and so forceful that Pilate removed the shields from the city, although he did so with ill grace. Later, he tried to bring shields with his name upon them into Jerusalem to hang in the praetorium. This, too, created an outcry and an appeal to Tiberius. He ordered Pilate to remove them and to hang them in Caesarea instead. That saved Jewish sensitivities and imperial honor at the same time.

At a later time, Pilate built an aqueduct to bring water to Jerusalem. Its major purpose was to serve the Temple area. He paid for this construction with the Temple treasures, which upset the Jews. Knowing of the abuse he would receive from the Jews when he appeared at the Temple, he sent soldiers into the Temple area in disguise. When he appeared, the Jews lashed out at him. At his signal, the soldiers retaliated, inflicting much injury and death. The resistance was crushed, but hatred of Pilate grew. He was described by Josephus as being guilty of "corruption, insults, rapine, outrages on the people, arrogance, repeated murders of innocent victims, and constant and most galling savagry."

The downfall of Pilate came about when a Samaritan prophet gathered the people of Samaria to Mount Gerizim, promising to reveal to them sacred vessels hidden there from the days of the conquest. Pilate, having been warned that a large crowd would be gathered, suspected them of planning an insurrection. His soldiers attacked the crowd and killed many people. This bloody act was reported to Vitellius, the legate of Syria. He ordered Pilate to Rome so that Tiberius could consider the case. Fortunately for Pilate, Tiberius died before he arrived in Rome. Numerous legends exist as to the fate of Pilate, but nothing is known with certainty.

After ordering Pilate to Rome, Vitellius appointed Marcellus as procurator in Pilate's place until the Roman emperor should act. Marcellus served only one year, AD 36. On the Feast of the Passover that year, Vitellius went to Jerusalem and won the favor of the Jews by remitting the taxes on fruit and releasing the garments of the high priest which the Romans had held since AD 6.

Upon the death of Tiberius, Caligula became emperor of Rome (AD 37-41). He appointed Marullus as procurator, whose term of office was the same as that of his master.

During the reign of Caligula, two major but related events took place which seriously disturbed Jewish life. First of all, a major outbreak of anti-Semitism took place in Alexandria. It clearly did so not only with imperial knowledge and permission but almost certainly with imperial urging. This went on for almost the entire period of Caligula's reign. The bloody pogrom in that city left a permanent mark upon the Jewish populace of Egypt. At the same time, possibly as an outgrowth of that experience and possibly as the cause of it, Caligula began to require worship of himself as a god. As a part of this, he ordered a statue of himself to be erected in Jerusalem. At this point, the new governor of Syria, Publius Petronius, who tried to be sensitive to the Jewish feelings, was beseiged by requests from the Jews to avoid erecting the statue. He tried every way possible to delay obeying the imperial order.

The events around the final authorization of this order are a bit confusing, but at last Caligula ordered the image to be placed in the Temple. Shortly thereafter, the emperor received a letter from Petronius urging that it not be done, insisting that nothing was to be gained. This so incensed the emperor that he sent a letter to his governor ordering him to commit suicide. However, not long afterward Caligula was murdered. The news of that murder reached Petronius before the final order to place the image in the Temple and commit suicide. Thus both he and the Jewish nation were spared that outrage. For the Jews of Judea, however, their experiences under these early procurators had certainly ended in turmoil. The procurators had brought no better time for them than the reign of the Herods.

Galilee and Perea: Herod Antipas (4 BC-AD 39)

In the disposition of the kingdom of Herod the Great, Galilee and Perea were more fortunate than Samaria and Judea, though only slightly so. Antipas, who took the name Herod, was appointed by Augustus as tetrarch there. At the very least his lengthy reign gave that region a far greater stability than was experienced by their brothers in Jerusalem.

The region over which Herod Antipas ruled was fertile and fruitful. Galilee was inhabited by a people with a strong sense of personal independence. They were farmers by background and were little involved in the world affairs which shook the people of Judea.

Antipas was, like his father, a builder. He was also scheming and cunning. He is known in the New Testament simply as Herod. Jesus underscored his conniving nature when He called him "that fox" (Luke 13:32). Herod Antipas was also sensitive to the feelings of his people, joining in the appeal to Tiberius against Pilate for placing the shields in the Temple at Jerusalem.

Herod's most magnificent achievement was his building of the city of Tiberias on the shores of the Sea of Galilee. During construction, builders discovered that the new city was on the site of an ancient graveyard. Since the Jews could have nothing to do with the dead lest it make them unclean, Herod had to populate his city with foreigners. This may have helped him avoid many of the direct conflicts which would have occurred if his capital had been populated with Jews.

When he met the wife of his brother Herod Philip in Rome, he fell under her power. He promised to marry her and returned home to divorce his wife, the daughter of the king of Nabateans, Aretas. She fled to her father. This dishonor obviously enraged her father. It proved to be the beginning of a series of conflicts on Herod's Perean border for the rest of his rule.

Undaunted, however, Herod married Herodias. She brought to his home her daughter, Salome. During this time, Herod, seeking to keep the peace in his land, had John the Baptist arrested. Outwardly, he may have feared John's arousing the populace. Inwardly, he clearly feared John's attacks on his morality. Following Salome's famous dance, Herod had John beheaded.

Herod was also significantly involved in the trial of Jesus. He had heard of the preaching of this Galilean Rabbi and feared that He might have been John the Baptist come to life again. (Such is the terror of a guilty conscience.) Also, Herod had also heard of Jesus' miracles and hoped to see some kind of performance. In this he was disappointed.

Herod had been significantly involved in the Parthian campaigns of Rome. When Agrippa I was made king over the region originally governed by his brother Philip, this stirred the envy of Herod's wife, Herodias. Thinking that Rome owed her husband a similar honor, she persuaded him to make an appeal to the emperor for elevation to the kingship. By the time he arrived in Rome, however, Caligula had received charges against Herod. When Herod could not successfully refute them, Caligula banished him to Gaul. In generosity, he offered to allow Herodias to live in Rome. However, she chose to accompany her husband into exile and in AD 39, the rule of Herod Antipas over Galilee came to an end.

Northern Transjordan: Philip (4 BC-AD 34)

The third of Herod's sons to succeed to part of his father's kingdom was Philip, who was named tetrarch of several small provinces northeast of the Sea of Galilee. In general, he was quite unlike either of his brothers or his father. As far as we have any record, not one single harsh judgment against or complaint about him was made by the people whom he governed or by the ancient writers who wrote of him or could have written of him.

Philip lived a generally quiet life. He married Salome, the daughter of his brother Herod Philip and later step-daughter of Herod Antipas. She was the one whose dance so impressed Antipas, that he promised her anything as a reward. Philip seldom left the boundaries of his territory, but travelled through it regularly. His major purpose in life was to keep the people of his kingdom happy and contented.

On his journeys through his provinces, he carried a portable throne with him. Wherever he came across a case which needed to be decided, he set up his throne and rendered immediate judgment. No accusation of either bribery or injustice was ever charged against him.

Philip did follow the family tradition of building. Two major cities are credited to him. He made his capital at the ancient site of Panias, rebuilding it and naming it Caesarea in honor of the Roman emperor. To distinguish it from other cities of that name, its full name was Caesarea Philippi. It is listed this way in the New Testament (Matt. 16:13; Mark 8:27). He also built a city in the neighborhood of the fishing village of Bethsaida, which he named Bethsaida Julias, in honor of the daughter of Augustus. This was a border city, just across the Jordan River from the major customs post of Capernaum.

Unlike the territories assigned to his two brothers, that assigned to Philip was not originally a part of the Jewish Land of Promise. It had no early tribal alignments and had been added to the territory of the Jews only during the days of the interbiblical era. The population of the region was primarily Gentile and was not as sensitive to the religious issues which so disturbed the people of Judea. Philip was the first ruler of the region to have an image of Caesar impressed upon his coins. He also had his own image stamped thereon. This would have created major problems elsewhere in the region, but apparently did not even raise an eyebrow in Philip's provinces.

The general peace and tranquility of the region over which Philip ruled made it an excellent place for Jesus to take His disciples when they needed to escape from the pressures and controversies of the regions of Galilee or Judea. Further, being primarily Gentile, it allowed a release from the constant Jewish publicity. It was well-governed and offered an escape from any threat of a violent attack. Finally, Jesus' presence there was not likely to foment any kind of political uprising.

Philip apparently had a very inquisitive mind; he was interested in the natural world around him. He would almost have fitted the modern definition of a scientist. The Jordan River was always supposed to have its source at Panias. Philip, however, threw chaff into a stream which disappeared into the ground at Phiale and discovered it surfacing at the supposed source of the Jordan at Panias, proving that its origin was elsewhere.

Because he had been a moderate and peace-loving ruler, Philip's death was deeply mourned by his people. He left no hostility and no inherent turmoil in his land. Following his death (AD 34), the territory which he governed was added to the province of Syria. It remained under Syrian control until the death of Tiberius in AD 37. At that time, Caligula made a different disposition of it.

Palestine to the First Jewish Revolt (AD 41-66)

Agrippa I, King

Aristobulus, the son of Herod the Great who was executed in 7 BC, was survived by several children. One of these was named Agrippa in honor of the Roman leader of that name who was a close friend of Aristobulus. Little Agrippa was four years old when his father was executed. Like many members of the family of Herod the Great, Agrippa was sent to Rome (along with his mother, Berenice) where he received the best of a Roman education. He also grew up as a friend and companion of several members of the emperor's family, being especially close to Caius.

Agrippa was an intemperate young man. He became so involved in debt that in AD 23 he was sent to Idumea, essentially in banishment. However, Herodias, the sister of Agrippa and the new wife of Herod Antipas, interceded for him. The result was that Agrippa was allowed to move to Tiberias, where he was given a home and an imperial pension. It wasn't long, however, before Agrippa had a major disagreement with his uncle Antipas and had to leave his territory. Finally, given permission to return to Rome, Agrippa in AD 36 went home to his beloved city. There, however, his fortunes did not improve. First, he plunged further into debt. Then he was overheard saying that he wished his friend Caius were emperor. Tiberius was enraged when he heard this and had Agrippa imprisoned. Agrippa's fortunes had gone from bad to worse. Death appeared to be imminent. And so it was, but for someone else. Tiberius died in AD 37.

Caius (Caligula) then became emperor. He immediately released Agrippa from prison. As a reward for Agrippa's wishing that Caligula should be emperor, Caligula appointed him king of the region of Philip, adding much of Syria to it. In addition, he took the iron fetters off of Agrippa and had a gold chain of equal weight forged for him as a reward. Agrippa's fortunes had truly turned! The Roman senate confirmed his appointment as king and elected him a Roman prefect as well.

In AD 39, as we have seen, Agrippa's sister Herodias, pushed her husband to appeal for a kingship like her brother's. Caligula instead banished him to Gaul. This left Galilee without a ruler. As a further bounty, in AD 40, Agrippa was named king of Judea and Perea.

During the early days of Agrippa's kingship, he served as a friend of the Jews who were being persecuted in Alexandria. In fact, his intercession brought them deliverance. Further, when Caligula sought to have his statue placed in the Jerusalem Temple, Agrippa journeyed to Rome to try to dissuade him. Agrippa succeeded, at least temporarily, in preventing that order from being fulfilled.

As a result of that journey, Agrippa was in Rome in January, AD 41, when Caligula was assassinated. He was influential, at least in some degree, in getting Claudius (Caligula's uncle) named emperor. As a reward, Claudius not only confirmed the appointments of Caligula but named Agrippa as king of Judea and Samaria as well. Thus, by AD 41, Agrippa ruled over as large or possibly a larger region than his grandfather Herod the Great.

When he returned to Palestine, Herod Agrippa (as he now called himself, being a part of the Herodian family) went to Jerusalem. Agrippa sought to strengthen the influence and power of Judea during his reign. However, Rome did not leave him much freedom of action. He was forced to stop building a fortifying wall north of the city and to disband a coalition of other regional kings which he had formed.

Agrippa immediately won the support of the Jewish leaders by making a thank offering, paying for the sacrifices of a number of Nazirites who were fulfilling their vows, and hanging the gold chain which Caligula had given him over the entrance to the Temple treasury. His piety was a source of satisfaction for many of the Jews. When his daughter was to marry a Gentile, Agrippa ordered him to be circumcised and become a Jew. So orthodox did Agrippa become that the Pharisees called him "Brother." The New Testament describes his eagerness to please the Jews by pointing to the martydom of James and the arrest of Peter (Acts 12:1-19).

Agrippa has been accused of being insincere and hypocritical in his piety. His early life showed no foundation for such piety. Further, outside of Judea, his rule showed little piety. Coins minted in Jerusalem bore no image, but those minted elsewhere not only had his image but a Roman name as well. Further, he was an ardent supporter of Hellenistic causes outside Judea. Inside Judea, however, he was a model of piety and modesty. The Pharisees, however, saw only what they wished to see and acclaimed him as their patron.

Herod Agrippa was survived by three daughters and a seventeen-year-old son, also named Agrippa, later to be known as Agrippa II. Claudius, the Roman emperor, planned to name him king in his father's place. However, upon the advice of his councillors, he changed his mind and reinstituted the administration of Palestine by procurators, reassigning the province to the regional administration of Syria.

The Roman Procurators

Two problems immediately asserted themselves when Claudius reimposed Roman administrators over the Jews. First, with the exception of the first two procurators, they showed utter insensitivity to the Jewish religious concerns. It is almost as if they were organized into a concerted effort to force the Jews into a revolt. As rulers, they were utterly inept. The second problem was that the Jews, having had a happy albeit a brief experience with a Jewish ruler, faced the renewed coming of foreign administrators not only without enthusiasm but without even an acceptance of the unavoidable. Viewed from either the position of the Roman governors or that of the Jewish leaders, from AD 44 onward open revolt moved rapidly from possible to probable to inevitable.

The first procurator of this period was Cuspius Fadus, who served from AD 44-46. He insisted that he had the right to keep the custody of the high priestly robes and to appoint the high priest. However, with a sense of justice, he allowed the Jews to appeal to Caesar. Through the mediation and influence of young Agrippa, this right was assigned at first to his brother Herod, king of Chalcis. Following his death in AD 48, it was then assigned to Agrippa himself (AD 49).

Fadus was also involved in a quick and brutal assault upon Theudas, a pretended messiah. Sensing, rightly so, that Theudas was about to start a revolt, Fadus attacked Theudas's supporters with cavalry. A number of rebels were killed or captured, and Theudas was beheaded. The grisly trophy was carried to Jerusalem as an object lesson and a threat to other would-be rebels. (This Theudas is not the same one mentioned in Acts 5:36 who carried out a revolt in the days following Herod's death in 4 BC).

Following Fadus, Tiberius Alexander served as procurator from AD 46-48. He was a Jew from Alexandria, a son of one of the leading families and a nephew of the famous philosopher Philo. However, he had renounced Judaism when he took service with the Romans. Although we have no record of it, his renunciation of the faith of his fathers must have seriously alienated the Jews of Jerusalem and Judea. During his term of service, he had to deal with a revolt led by James and Simon, two sons of Judas the Galilean Zealot who had revolted at the occasion of the census in AD 6. When these two sons were captured and crucified, the revolt was thoroughly put down. The crucifixion of two "loyal" Jews by an apostate would have further created hostility among the populace. A severe famine is recorded during this time. It is almost certainly the one when the church of Antioch sent relief to Jerusalem by Barnabas and Paul (Acts 11:28-30).

Times were difficult under the administration of these first two procurators. They became impossible with their successors. Alexander was succeeded by Ventidius Cumanus, who served from AD 48-52. Almost immediately, troubles began. At the Passover, when the Roman soldiers were stationed in Jerusalem, one made an insulting gesture to the Jewish worshipers. This so aroused them that Cumanus called in his troops to restore the peace. A stampede to escape their swords began and, by the end, some twenty to thirty thousand people were killed. Shortly thereafter, a Roman was beaten and robbed near Jerusalem. In retaliation, Roman troops looted the nearby villages. During the looting, a soldier found a copy of the Torah and publicly tore it up. However, for this extreme provocation, Cumanus executed the soldier.

A third situation arose when a group of Galilean pilgrims going to Jerusalem for a festival were murdered as they passed through Samaria.

Cumanus, accepting a bribe from the Samaritans, did nothing. At this point, a band of Zealots invaded Samaria, murdering everyone they could find, from infants to the aged. In turn, Cumanus's soldiers attacked the Zealots, killing some and taking others prisoner. All groups complained to Quadatus, the governor of Syria. Following his investigation, he sent his report, along with Cumanus, the Jewish leaders, and the Samaritans to Rome to stand trial before Claudius. Agrippa was in Rome at that time and interceded for the Jews. They were freed. The Samaritans were executed, and Cumanus was removed from office for having accepted the bribe.

Following Cumanus's removal, Antonius Felix (known in the New Testament simply as Felix) was appointed procurator (AD 52-60). He apparently was a nominee suggested by the Jewish high priest and had served as an aide to Cumanus in Samaria. He was a freedman, a former slave of Antonia who was the mother of Claudius. Such an appointment with such broad powers was unusual, if not unprecedented. Felix's administration firmly solidified Jewish opposition to Rome. Tacitus evaluated him by saying: "Practising every kind of cruelty and lust, he wielded royal power with the instincts of a slave." (Schurer, vol. 1, p. 461.) He was married three times, and one of his wives was Drusilla, the sister of Agrippa II. He took her from her husband, the king of Emesa. His public life was no better than his private life, for he took what he wished and did what he pleased, caring little for the law and less for public opinion.

Because of his mismanagement, misgovernment, and open disdain for public sentiment, the party of the Zealots increased rapidly, both in numbers and in public support. They confined their robberies and attacks to political opponents, indicating that, while they were bandits, they were also patriots. Felix struck at them with severity and cruelty. At first, he was somewhat successful. However, his success caused the creation of a subgroup of Zealots. These were primarily political assassins. They mingled with large crowds and quietly stabbed to death the Jewish leaders who had collaborated with the Romans. Their daggers were called *sica* and this group came to be known as the sicarii. Felix once collaborated with them to arrange the assassination of the high priest Jonathan. He had first nominated Felix to be procurator. Due to the excesses of Felix, Jonathan had become a critical opponent, and Felix found this an expedient way to have the priest removed. Because of the sicarii, assassination became quite common in Jerusalem. No leader felt safe in a crowd.

Added to the political radicals were the religious ones. Josephus described them as having "cleaner hands but wickeder intentions" (*Wars of the Jews*, II, 13). They incited religious fervor in anticipation of the kingdom of God which was to be brought in through the process of finding freedom through casting off the Roman yoke. One of these, an Egyptian, is mentioned in Acts 21:38. Felix dealt with him in his usual swift and overpowering way, slaughtering all the followers whom he could get his hands on. The Egyptian, however, escaped. Some of his followers saw his deliverance as miraculous and expected equally as miraculous a return (as Acts 21:38 apparently indicates).

However, Felix's swift action, instead of putting an end to the problems, merely intensified them. The religious and political fanatics found common cause and united. They formed roving bands which swept through the countryside pillaging, looting, murdering, and burning houses and villages.

In addition to these external problems, the priesthood fell into internal conflict. The high priests, their supporters, and servants were at odds with other priests. Those stationed at the Temple stole the tithes which belonged to the others, leaving many to starve to death.

During this time of intense unrest, Paul was imprisoned in Jerusalem (Acts 23—24). When he had an opportunity to speak to Felix and Drusilla, he spoke of what he thought they most needed to hear, of righteousness, justice, chastity, and future judgment.

During the latter days of Felix's administration, riots broke out in Caesarea. The Jews and the Syrians each claimed precedence of citizenship. When Felix responded with violence, the riots were not quelled but grew. Felix finally arrested the leaders and sent them to Rome. However, Nero also recalled him because of his inability to control the situation.

Nero then sent a new procurator, Porcius Festus (AD 60-62). Shortly after Festus's arrival, word also arrived from Nero that the Gentiles (Syrians) in that city had priority of citizenship. In the eyes of the Jews, this reduced them to second-class citizens. This was bad enough, but the fact that this decision had been reached by bribing Nero's secretary made the Jewish reaction worse. The activities of the sicarii increased, and a new messiah led multitudes into the desert in preparation for the coming of the kingdom. Festus acted swiftly and violently. That problem was ended, but others cropped up. During this period, he had numerous conversations with Paul. Finally, at his own request as a Roman citizen, Paul was sent to Nero (Acts 24:11 *ff.*).

At one point in Festus's administration, a dispute arose between Agrippa II and the Jerusalem priesthood. Agrippa added a tower to his

Jerusalem home which overlooked the Temple area. The priests in return built a high wall to block his view. Agrippa appealed to Festus, who ordered the wall to be demolished. The Jews then appealed to Nero. Nero's wife, Poppaea, interceded with the emperor, and the Jews received permission to let the wall remain. The whole situation added fuel to the fires of unrest.

Festus died suddenly, leaving a vacancy. In the three months before a successor arrived, the region was ruled by anarchy. The high priest settled some old scores by having numerous people arrested, tried by the Sanhedrin, and executed. This only served further to aggravate the turmoil. Agrippa II stepped in (he had the power of appointing the high priest), removed Annas II, and replaced him with Jesus son of Damnaeus. The followers of the two rivals engaged in street fighting.

At this point, Albinus, the new procurator arrived. He served AD 62-64. His primary motivation appears to have been greed. He accepted bribes from the supporters of both high priests as well as from the sicarii, and then let them all do as they pleased. He gave the appearance of dealing with the unrest by massive arrests. But anyone so arrested could then buy his freedom. The sicarii, however, discovered a better way. They simply captured pro-Romans and traded them to Albinus for the freedom of their own people. Anarchy became the rule of the day. No longer was any room left in Jerusalem for moderates or middle-of-the-roaders. People were forced to take a side. The anti-Roman forces grew in numbers and strength. The situation was totally out of hand. It is doubtful that anyone could have brought it under control. Certainly a man with the venality of Albinus could not.

In AD 64 Albinus was recalled, and Gessius Florus (AD 64-66) was appointed. He apparently was appointed, not because of any ability, but because his wife was a close friend of Nero's wife. Florus was so greedy and so willing to accept bribes that his predecessor appeared like a saint in comparison. He was clearly the worst of a bad lot. He plundered villages and cities and allowed any thief to practice his trade as long as the procurator got his share. His rule was the last straw. The opposition to the Romans was at white heat. War was inevitable. No other outcome was possible.

Agrippa II (AD 49-ca. 92)

As we have seen, when Herod Agrippa died, he was survived by a seventeen-year-old son, Agrippa II. Though educated in Rome and a friend of Claudius, he was denied the throne of Judea because of Rome's inherent fear of hereditary monarchies. However, in AD 49, he was appointed king of Chalcis, a small kingdom to the north of Palestine. At the same time, he was given the authority of appointing high priests in Jerusalem. In AD 53, the territory of Philip was also given to him, and shortly thereafter much of Galilee and Perea were added. His personal morality was the source of many problems to the Jews, as his sister Berenice frequently lived with him.

Agrippa II was first, last, and always a loyal supporter of Rome and Roman policy. He maintained fairly good relations with the high priests of Jerusalem. This was probably due to the fact that they held their office at his pleasure. Near the end of the period of the Roman procurators, however, there was a major split over his tower and their wall. Ultimately, he sought to prevent the Jewish revolt. When it came, however, he was unquestionably on the side of the Romans. After the revolt, we hear almost nothing of him. He died about AD 92.

The Significance of the Period

Christianity

To the Christian, the most signifcant feature of the era from the death of Herod the Great (4 BC) to the First Jewish Revolt (AD 66) is Jesus and the ministry of His disciples. However, outside the New Testament itself, the world took little notice and kept few records of the events reported in the New Testament. The birth of a son to a carpenter and his wife (as such would have appeared) from Nazareth in the village of Bethlehem would have gone, and did go, unnoticed and unrecorded in either Jerusalem or Rome. The crucifixion as a common criminal of that same person slightly more than three decades later also went unrecorded in Rome, where so-called bigger things demanded governmental attention. Further, the spread of a message of resurrection and redemption throughout the empire was hardly noticed until the end of this era. Were it not for the conflicts between the Jews and the Christians and the burning of Rome and its resulting blame on the Christians by Nero, we would have almost no mention at all in Roman annals of the early Christians. Yet of all the events of this seventy-year era, not one had the ultimate impact upon the world as did the birth, life, death, and resurrection of Jesus of Nazareth.

The Parties

During this era, only four Jewish parties were of any major significance. The people at Qumran withdrew more as the world around them became increasingly turbulent. Rather than turning outward, they turned inward, studying and preserving God's Word. They looked for better days to be brought in by God, and they waited with patience. Their attitude toward the Roman conquerors, the Jewish leaders, or the Zealot patriots was simply: "A plague on all your *houses.*"

On the other hand, the Zealots became stronger and more active. As the corruption of political leaders drove them to despair, they sought deliverance by their own hand. Their every action was intended to free their land from the Roman rule. Unfortunately, they, too, practiced excesses. They took up the sword with one commitment, victory or death. Their ultimate belief was that there was no room in Palestine for Romans and Jews. No path for the Zealots led to any kind of coexistence. For them, the ultimate issues had become quite simple. Rome had to go.

Between these extremes were the Pharisees and Sadducees. As in the preceding periods, the Sadducees remained the party of wealth and power. They controlled the high priesthood by collaborating with Rome as far as possible and paying large sums into the Roman coffers. To pay these sums, they had to collect the funds from the people and did so in various oppressive ways. Facing the reality that Rome was in Judea to stay, the Sadducees sought to make the best of a bad situation. Accepting Rome's presence, they sought to and did prosper from it.

The Pharisees, on the other hand, were generally not collaborators. They turned their concerns to the Law and to its practical application. During the brief reign of Herod Agrippa I, they had sensed a golden age. Unfortunately for them, it did not last. The oppressive and foolish tactics of the Roman administrators drove them, if not into active support of the Zealots, at least into passive support. When the Romans finally made it impossible for them to be orthodox, the breach was complete.

The Sanhedrin

This name came to be used of the assembly of Jewish elders and religious leaders about 63 BC. During the reign of Herod the Great (37-4 BC), the Sanhedrin had little or no influence. When Rome took over the administration of Jerusalem and Judea, however, its power increased.

The Sanhedrin could pronounce judgment as a court in matters of religious as well as secular cases. However, no important decision could be carried out without the subsequent approval of the Roman procurators. The Sanhedrin was also intended to interpret and apply the Torah.

Apparently the Sanhedrin was made up of senior priests (generally Sadducees) and scribes and elders (generally Pharisees). We do not know of the numerical relationship between the two groups. However, as the high priest always presided over it, it would appear that the Sadducees generally controlled it.

The Scribes

Scribes are heard of as early as the time of Ezra and Nehemiah. However, they really came into prominence in the era which we have considered in this chapter. Their Hebrew name was *sopherim*. Literally, anyone who could write was a scribe. However, the term had developed a technical meaning by the New Testament era so that it was applied to those who studied, preserved, passed on, and expounded the Word of God. They were the keepers of the tradition. In this era, they were still distinct from the Pharisees, although sharing much in common. Some scribes were Pharisees, but not all. The foundation of the development of the rabbis appears to be found in these scribes of the New Testament era.

Historical Issues

The attitudes of the Jews toward the Romans and of the Romans toward the Jews solidified in this era. The Romans despised the Jews as hardheaded, unreasonable, stiff-necked, and reactionary. The Jews saw the Romans as godless, brutal, corrupt, and oppressive. The Jews and the Romans spoke to one another but never heard each other. Each consciously and intentionally offended the other and then took offense themselves at the other's offense. It is difficult if not impossible to determine the "what ifs" of history. What if the Jews had tried harder to get along with Rome? What if Rome had sought to understand the Jews and rule them sympathetically? To neither of these questions do we have answers. The only thing we know is that history shows these two nations to have had irreconcilable differences. The Jewish revolts may have been inevitable from the day Pompey set foot in Jerusalem. It is certain that, given the procurators Rome sent, from the time Fadus arrived in Judea (AD 44) the days of the Jewish state were numbered. An object which wished to be immovable was about to be crushed by a force which was irresistible.

The Chronology of Christianity

Although I have indicated that this chapter is in no way an attempt to write a history of Christianity, it would be a disservice to the student not to point out how the major events of the New Testament fit into the era.

The birth of Jesus did not occur at what we now call the beginning of the Christian era. We know that the monk (Dionysius Exiguus) who originally calculated this in the sixth century AD made a four-year error. Jesus had to have been born while Herod the Great was still king, for the Wise Men sought him out in their search for the infant "king of the Jews" (Matt. 2:1). Since Herod died in 4 BC, Jesus' birth could have been no later. It may have been earlier since Herod ordered the execution of all male children two or under. However, that is another issue.

We do know approximately when Jesus began His ministry. The beginning of the ministry of John the Baptist is dated quite precisely to the "fifteenth year of the reign of Tiberius Caesar" (Luke 3:1 *ff.*). Sometime shortly thereafter, Jesus went to John to be baptized, being "about thirty years at age" (v. 23). If this occurred in the same year, since Tiberius began to reign in AD 14, Jesus' ministry must have begun about AD 29/30.

Dating Jesus' crucifixion is another matter. Pilate was procurator at the time, and he served from AD 26 to AD 36. Tradition ascribes a three-year ministry to Jesus, but John's Gospel appears to refer to at least three and possibly four Passovers. If His ministry included four Passovers, the crucifixion would have occurred about AD 34. That is at least a possible though by no means a certain interpretation. It could have been earlier but almost certainly no later.

The next event which can be established is the date of James' execution and Peter's imprisonment. Since that occurred at the Passover shortly before the death of Herod Antipas (cf. Acts 12), it must be placed at Passover in AD 39.

The last New Testament date which can be established with any degree of certainty by correlation with external events is the time of Paul's ministry. Paul was in Corinth when Gallio was proconsul. He was arrested in Jerusalem during the time of the procuratorship of Felix (AD 52-60) and remained in prison until the time of Festus (AD 60-62). Gallio was in Corinth in the year of AD 50-51. Paul was brought before him at that time (Acts 18:12). Thus, we can fix Paul's presence in Corinth at that time. He apparently left shortly thereafter. Felix imprisoned Paul for two years (Acts 24:27). Under the procuratorship of Festus, Paul appealed to Caesar and was sent to Rome (25:11-12). Paul could have sailed for Rome no earlier than AD 60, the year of Festus's appointment. He must have been arrested sometime in AD 58. Of his death we know nothing. He went to Rome while Nero was emperor (AD 54-68). Tradition ascribes Paul's death to the reign of that evil man, and there is no significant reason to doubt it.

9
The End of the Hebrew State
(AD 66-135)

The sad story of Judea swept to its end in the period from AD 66 to AD 135. Some nations die quietly, simply being assimilated into those which succeed them on the stage of history. Others die violently, being carried kicking and screaming from a stage which they do not wish to leave. Such was the fate of Judea. Conceived in the pilgrimage of Abraham from Ur and born in the miraculous deliverance of slaves from Egypt, the Hebrew nation was crushed by the might of Rome. It is difficult to decide if its fate was murder or suicide. The events of history appear to support either conclusion.

Chronological Table
The Final Days of the Hebrew Nation (AD 66-135)

Rome	Palestine
Nero (54-68)	First Jewish Revolt (66-74)
	Vespasian conquers Galilee, (67),
Galba (68-69)	Perea, and part of Judea (68)
Otho (69)	
Vitellius (69)	Jerusalem falls (70)
	Brassus, Governor (71-73)
Vespasian (69-79)	Silva, Governor (73-81)
	Fall of Masada (74)
	The period of Jabneh (74-132)
	Johanan ben Zakkai (74-80)
Titus (79-81)	Gamaliel II (80-120)

Domitian (81-96)

Persecution of Christians (96)

Nerva (96-98)

Trajan (98-117)   Quietus, governor (117)

Hadrian (117-138)   Bar Kochba Revolt (132-135)

Fall of Bethar (135)

The Affairs in Rome

The reign of Nero moved swiftly to an end following the fire in Rome and the persecution of the Christians in AD 64. A conspiracy to assassinate the emperor failed in AD 65. This, however, resulted in the heightening of his rule of terror. Yet the end was in sight. He had created influential and powerful enemies. Once again, the Praetorian Guard took the lead and declared their support for Galba, who was in Spain, as emperor. Realizing all was lost, Nero fled from Rome and committed suicide in AD 68.

Galba, supported by Otho, declared himself emperor and marched into Rome in October, AD 68. However, the situation got out of hand. The Praetorians murdered their commander and their support began to wane. Every act of Galba appears to have alienated someone. As a result, Vitellius, sent by Galba to lead the legions in the Germanic regions, was acclaimed emperor by his troops in January AD 69. In the meantime, Otho led a revolt of the Praetorians, assassinated Galba, and was also proclaimed emperor. When Otho's and Vitellius's forces met in battle in April AD 69, Otho was overcome and committed suicide.

Hearing of this victory, Vitellius rushed from Germany and marched on Rome. He foolishly humiliated the defeated army of Otho when he arrived in July. In the meantime, Vespasian turned from his campaign in Judea. He had originally supported Galba and then Otho. Now, however, he had personal ambitions. After a number of campaigns, Vitellius was murdered; Vespasian marched into Rome and was proclaimed emperor, starting a new dynasty. (The emperor's full name was Titus Flavius Vespasianus and the line which he founded is called the Flavian emperors.) Thus AD 69, the year of the four emperors, came to an end. Rome had never experienced such a year. The government was impoverished by the chaos and conflict. Vespasian wisely raised taxes to replenish the treasury. He began foolishly extravagant building projects, the most famous of which was the Colosseum. As a successful soldier, he was respected by the military leaders of his day and restored discipline throughout the army.

Vespasian was untrained and unprepared for the leadership of an empire, but he did a remarkable job of administration. He was a hard worker and was not the victim of pampered upbringing. Uncultured by Roman standards, he was rough and honest. He was truly mourned at his death in AD 79.

Titus (AD 79-81) succeeded his father to the throne. He had been associated with him closely both as a military commander in Judea and as a political ruler in Rome. His brief reign was remembered for his generosity and for its peace.

Upon the death of Titus, his brother Domitian succeeded to the throne (AD 81-96). Because he was utterly afraid of opposition, he took refuge in declaring himself to be divine and called himself *Dominus et Deus noster* (Our Lord and God). Fearful of those who sought answers to questions, in both AD 89 and AD 95 he exiled all philosophers from Rome. Further, Domitian's relations with the senate steadily declined. Leaders of Rome were persecuted and executed during the latter years of his rule, which gave rise to the legend of *Nero redivivus* (Nero come back to life). Jews were the special subject of his hatred, and he exacted the Temple tax from them in spite of the fact that the Temple had been destroyed more than two decades earlier. Scattered but intense persecution of Christians was also carried out at the end of his reign.

Domitian was assassinated in AD 96 and was the last of the Flavian emperors. He was succeeded by Cocceius Nerva, a descendent of an old family of Roman nobility. He ruled with a deliberate policy of reconciliation and restoration of Rome's economy. Though motivated by good intentions, Nerva was simply too old (d. AD 98) and ruled too briefly to bring much restoration to the empire. Perhaps his greatest accomplishment was the selection of Ulpius Trajanus (Trajan) as his successor.

After Trajan died in AD 117, his nephew Publius Aelius Hadrianus, whom we know as Hadrian, became emperor (AD 117-138). Hadrian was governor of Syria when he was named emperor. He made several extensive tours of the empire. In Britain in AD 122 he established the frontier barrier known as Hadrian's Wall. During his reign he visited Africa, Egypt, Judea, Syria, Greece, and Asia Minor. These visits allowed him to organize his administration and to strengthen his military control. He was also a patron of the arts. Because he was an extreme egoist, the end of his reign was marred by the execution of those whom he suspected of treason toward himself. Before his death in AD 138 the Jewish state had come to its final tragic end.

The Jewish Revolts

The First Jewish Revolt

All sorts of reasons for the First Jewish Revolt have been given. The deep-seated reason was hatred between the two groups, Judeans and Romans. The immediate causes, however, can be found in Casarea and Jerusalem. Nero's decision about citizenship had relegated the Jews in Caesarea to a second-class status in AD 66. To add insult to injury, some of the Gentiles sacrificed a bird in front of the synagogue at Caesarea. This made the synagogue unclean and implied that the Jews were lepers, for such a sacrifice was a part of the ritual for the cure of leprosy. The Jews of Caesarea appealed to the procurator Florus and offered him a bribe. He took the bribe and ignored their complaint.

This bribe may have put ideas into the procurator's head, however, for he then went to Jerusalem and took seventeen talents from the Temple treasury. Pilate had done the same, but he at least had an excuse. Florus had no excuse. In mockery of the poverty of their procurator, the Jews took up a public offering for him. This so incensed Florus that he sent his soldiers into the city to loot and kill. The Jews reacted so violently that these troops had to be withdrawn to Caesarea. One cohort took refuge in the Fortress of Antonia, but the Jews kept them isolated there.

At this point Agrippa II tried to persuade the Jewish leaders to restore the peace. The legate of Syria sent a tribune to investigate and the city remained calm while he was there. But the die had been cast. Shortly afterward Eleazar, son of the high priest and captain of the Temple guard, persuaded the priests to accept no offerings from aliens. This in effect abolished the required daily sacrifice on behalf of Caesar and was an insult Rome could not abide. The Zealots added a military insult as well, attacking the Roman troops at Masada, killing them all, and occupying the fortress themselves. The Zealots then moved into Jerusalem and burned the palaces of Agrippa II and the high priest, as well as other homes of the wealthy. They then drove the Romans from the Antonia, and Jerusalem was at last free from Roman occupation.

Fighting broke out throughout the land, particularly in the cities of mixed population. Jews were massacred in Gentile cities, and Gentiles were treated the same in Jewish cities. Atrocities abounded on every hand. In the fall of AD 66, Cestus Gallus, the governor of Syria, marched into Judea. He was beaten back from Jerusalem and suffered a shattering defeat when his army was ambushed at Beth-horon.

At this point, the Jewish leaders of Jerusalem realized that they needed to prepare for war. Flavius Josephus was elected by the Sanhedrin as commander of the Jewish troops in Galilee, for the Roman attack had to come from that direction. Josephus immediately began to gather and train an army, as well as to fortify several major Galilean cities, including Jotapata. The Zealots, however, suspected Josephus of being more concerned with making peace with Rome than with defending Galilee. We do not know whether their leader, John of Gischala, had reason to suspect Josephus, though future events clearly justified his suspicions. An attempt was made to assassinate Josephus, but it failed. Further, the people of the cities in Galilee were generally supportive of Rome while those of the towns and villages were more nationalistic. All of this seriously upset Josephus's preparations.

Meanwhile, when Nero heard of the Jewish revolt, he ordered General Vespasian to restore order. Cestus, who had been beaten so badly at Beth-horon, had died apparently by suicide. Vespasian marched with two legions, gathered a third commanded by his son Titus from Egypt, and added other contingents along the way. Advance elements of his army had experienced some victories in AD 66, but in AD 67 Vespasian besieged Jotapata. It fell violently after forty-seven days. Josephus and a number of his followers hid in a cave, vowing suicide before capture. However, Josephus escaped when the others died and surrendered to Vespasian. When he was brought before Vespasian, the Hebrew general predicted that the Roman would soon be emperor. Vespasian was pleased, and Josephus immediately became a Roman protege. There is some reason for believing that Josephus betrayed his fortress and his troops into the hands of the Romans.

Vespasian's army quickly moved through Galilee, having wholly overrun it by the end of AD 67. In the next year, Perea, Idumea, and part of Judea were in his hands. When Galilee had fallen, John of Gischala, the Zealot leader, had escaped to Jerusalem. Several rivals were seeking to lead the Jewish forces, but by early AD 68 John was firmly in control. In that year, the last high priest entered into office in Jerusalem; he did so under the patronage of the Zealot leader. Phinehas, appointed to this post, was not of the leading priestly families but was a rural priest who had been chosen by lot.

By late spring AD 68, all was set for a showdown. Jerusalem was firmly under Zealot control, led by John, and Vespasian's troops were marching toward it, preparing to besiege it. However, at that time Nero committed suicide to escape execution and Rome itself was in turmoil as rivals struggled over the succession. Vespasian suspended military operations to see how it would all turn out. The Jews in Jerusalem saw this as a divine intervention to deliver them. Their respite was short-lived, however. By AD 69 Vespasian was on the move again. In the meantime, three rivals attempted to control the Jewish forces in Jerusalem. Their inner struggle further weakened the defense of the city.

At this point, Vespasian was named emperor and left his forces to go to Rome. He turned his command over to his son Titus. At Passover in AD 70, the Jews were still confident of Jerusalem's deliverance and throngs came to celebrate Passover. Their presence added to the problems of food and water. Meanwhile, the internal struggles among the rivals led to further problems, such as supplies of food being burned lest the other faction eat it. The Romans invaded the city, and their crushing advance upon the Temple proceeded street by street. Violence and bloodshed were the rule of the day. Cannibalism was practiced by the defenders in order to survive. Finally the Temple fell in AD 70, was totally burned, and the ruins pulled down. Judea was no longer free.

Although the revolt, to all intents and purposes, was over, three fortress continued to resist. Herodium fell in AD 71 and Machaerus in AD 72. Masada, however, was a different matter. Defended since AD 66 by Zealots under the leadership of Eleazar, the grandson of Judas the Galilean, it had been well-fortified and well-supplied. The Romans had no easy time of it, but the citadel fell in AD 74. When the Romans finally entered it, they found only two women and five children who had survived the last suicide pact. Even the Romans were appalled at such commitment.

Judea was then occupied by the Romans and was made into a senatorial province. Peace, such as it was, was restored. The harsh power of Rome was seen and felt on every hand. The revolt was over, and its cost had been astronomical.

The Interim (AD 74-132)

The most significant development in the interim between the two Jewish revolts was the rise of rabbinic Judaism. The Pharisees and the scribes were the only two groups or parties to survive the First Jewish Revolt. And even the name, "Pharisee," gradually disappears from the literature after AD 70. The survivors of these two groups were among the rabbis who began to spring up at this time. This title showed up as *rab* ("teacher") or *rabbi* ("my teacher"). However, with the passage of time, rabbi simply became a synonym for "teacher." Following the destruction of the Temple, the rabbis sought to establish means by which their faith might survive. They found this, in the tradition of Pharisee and scribe, through the study of the Scriptures and its application to life. They sought not only to teach the Scripture by word but to live out its implications and applications.

During the siege of Jerusalem, probably during the lull in the contest for the emperorship, a rabbi named Johanan ben Zakkai had been allowed by Vespasian to flee the city and to settle in Jamnia (Jabneh), a place located south of Jaffa. There he set up a school which became a major center of rabbinic Judaism. Others seem to have done the same thing in Tiberias and Tel Aviv. However, the center at Jabneh became the more important. In Jabneh, the Beth Din ("House of judgment" or "Court of judgment") was established as the successor to the Sanhedrin. The leadership of this school and the Beth Din passed from Johanan to Gamaliel II, about AD 80. He continued to lead until AD 120.

One of the major contributions of the school at Jamnia was the rabbinic council (or councils) which sought to determine the Jewish canon of the Old Testament. The first of these was held about AD 96. We cannot be certain when the canon was finally settled, but it appears most likely to have occurred about the time of the Second Jewish Revolt (AD 132-135).

Finally, during the interim between the two revolts, the synagogue movement got its biggest push. Synagogues probably originated during the time of the Babylonian captivity. They were established to teach and study the Scriptures and to furnish a worship center other than the Temple in Jerusalem. Julius Caesar had established Judaism as a *religio licta,* a permitted or licensed religion. This was still in effect and allowed the establishment of synagogue worship centers wherever Jews were found. The new rabbinic movement furnished leaders for these synagogues. Taken together and from a human standpoint, it was the growth of synagogues and the development of rabbinism which allowed Judaism to survive as a living religion.

The Second Jewish Revolt (AD 132-135)

The underlying causes of the second revolt, as well as the details, are not as well-known as are those of the first. Three causes are suggested by the very scarce literature of the era. First, a Jewish tradition claims that Hadrian visited Judea and promised to rebuild the Temple. This may have served as an impetus to the rise of renewed nationalism. However, due to the problems which the Romans had had with Judea, it is highly questionable that any rebuilding of the Temple would have been allowed, much less instigated, by a Roman emperor. On the other hand, such a promise on the part of Hadrian could have fitted well with his general emphasis on conciliation. We simply cannot confirm this tradition.

The second and third causes suggested for the revolt were the announced plan to rebuild Jerusalem as a Gentile city named Aelia Capitolina and the forbidding of circumcision. Either of these surely would have aroused hostility and provoked a rebellion. On the other hand, both of these measures sound like what a ruler like Hadrian would have done in response to and retaliation for the revolt. All that we can say is that any of these are possibilities, none are certainties.

Whatever the cause, the revolt broke out in AD 132 under the leadership of Bar Kochba, as he is called by the Christian sources, or Ben or Bar Kozeba or Koziba as he was called by the rabbis. The first name means "Son of the Star" and the second is "Son of the Lie." We know nothing of his heritage. On some of the coins minted at the time he was called "Prince *[nasi]* of Israel." That term was normally applied to the president of the Beth Din. Those who held that title and position at this time seem to have all been descendants of Rabbi Hillel. However, we have no way of knowing whether the title carries that significance on these coins.

According to the rabbinic literature, when the revolt broke out in AD 132, Rabbi Akiba claimed that its leader, Simon, was the fulfillment of the messianic hope expressed in Numbers 24:17-18.

> A star shall come forth out of Jacob,
>   and a scepter shall rise out of Israel:
> it shall crush the forehead of Moab,
>   and break down all the sons of Sheth.
> Edom shall be dispossessed
>   Seir also, his enemies shall be dispossessed,
> while Israel does valiantly.

This was especially significant to Akiba, for by this time the rabbis saw the Old Testament Edom as the symbol for Rome. This was interpreted as predicting victory over Rome. Thus Simon came to be called Bar

Kochba, "Son of the Star." However, the rabbinic literature was written after the end of the revolt, and his utter defeat caused him to be there called Bar Kozeba, "Son of the Lie."

Whatever the cause, when the revolt began it spread rapidly. It appears doubtful that it went as far as Galilee, Perea, or Samaria. However, it clearly included most, if not all, of Judea. In general, many historians consider this to be the most terrible struggle in which the Jews were ever engaged. As the revolt spread, more and more people rallied to its support. The initial victories were due to surprise and to the small number of Roman troops in the area at that time.

For all of his emphasis upon conciliation, Hadrian could not allow a revolt against imperial authority to succeed. Thus he ordered one of his better generals, Severus, to put it down. The early successes of Bar Kochba are borne witness to by the coins which were minted and dated according to the years of the "Freedom of Israel" or the "Freedom of Jerusalem."

When the Roman troops marched into Judea, the conflict intensified and was fought with an unprecedented bitterness. The Romans listed 50 fortresses and 985 fortified villages which had to be taken separately. The toll of the dead is said to have reached 850,000 people. The Romans, while victorious, must have suffered severe losses in the three-year conflict. In Hadrian's reports to the senate, he consistently left out the traditional phrase: "All is well with me and my legions."

But if conditions were bad for the Romans, they were worse for the Jews. Having been driven from their fortresses, the Jews turned the war into a guerrilla conflict, centered in the hill country and the wilderness. Severus pursued them into caves, barricaded them, and starved them out. The final battle was fought at the fortress of Bethar, the last bastion of the rebels. It finally fell in AD 135 with bloody excesses. Mopping-up, however, continued in the caves and ravines for some months. Bar Kochba died at Bethar. Rabbi Akiba was brutally executed. Martyrs for the Jewish cause were executed on every hand, and Jews were carried off as slaves in uncounted numbers. So many were enslaved that it was said that in Rome's slave markets a Jewish slave cost only slightly more than a horse. Thus, in blood and suffering, the Second Jewish Revolt came to an end.

Final Developments

At the end of the revolt, Hadrian sought to eliminate the threat of any such event happening again. Jerusalem was turned into a Gentile city and renamed Aelia Capitolina. Jews were forbidden to enter the city on penalty of death. Circumcision was forbidden with the same penalty being imposed. Sabbath observance and reading of the Torah were also forbidden in Palestine. These restrictions were eased somewhat under the rule of Hadrian's successor, Antoninus Pius (AD 138-161). However, the prohibition against Jews entering their former capital remained in force. This was only eased slightly under the rule of Constantine in the fourth century when the Jews were allowed in once a year on the ninth of Ab to lament their lost home.

The end had come. The Jews had lost everything—home, possessions, land, and their religion (or so it appeared). They were ripped loose from the land of their heritage and became wanderers on the face of the earth. Yet they survived. Against all odds, they survived. In spite of all that had occurred and all that they had suffered, they survived. They survived with grief and sorrow, but also with a hope. Inexplicably, from a human standpoint, they looked to a future. With no land to unite them and hold them together, they were united and held together by synagogue and Torah.

A new era had dawned for the Jews with the end of the Second Jewish Revolt. They were a people without a country. The interbiblical period had truly ended. The events which began with Alexander in 333 BC and with Pompey in 63 BC had ground to their inexorable conclusion in AD 135. Jerusalem was dead, but the Jews continued. With no human reason to survive, they refused to die. The ultimate destruction of the Jewish state turned them into exiles, wanderers through the nations of the earth, looking and longing for the day they could return to Jerusalem.

For the early Christians, on the other hand, the destruction of the Jewish nation was not so traumatic. The earlier destruction of Jerusalem in the First Jewish Revolt (AD 66-70) had freed them once and for all from their ties to the Jerusalem church. They had become a faith with no geographic ties and with the world as its field. If anything, at that time Rome had become the Christians' major center. The final end of Judea and Jerusalem only prevented those who might look back from doing so. Instead of becoming wanderers, they became people on a mission. Instead of being exiles going *from* somewhere, they were pilgrims going *to* somewhere. They, too, had a hope, but what a different hope it was.

Appendix
Chronological Tables

The Rise of Greece (333-301 BC)

Alexander's campaigns (333-323)
    Battle of Issus (333)
    Tyre captured (332)
    Gaza captured (332)
    Alexandria founded in Egypt (331)
    Battle of Gaugamela (331)
Struggles of the Diadochi (323-301)
    Surreptitious conflict (323-ca.315)
    Ptolemy I controls Egypt (ca.323-283)
    Antigonus Monophthalmus in Palestine (ca. 320)
    Ptolemy attacks Jerusalem (312)
    Seleucus I captures Babylon (312)
    Antigonus captures Palestine (312)
    Battle of Ipsus (302)
    Ptolemy seizes Palestine (301)

The Ptolemaic Era (301-198 BC)

Egypt	Syria	High Priest
Ptolemy I Soter (323-283)	Seleucus I (312-281)	Onias I
		Simeon I Eleazar
Ptolemy II Philadelphus (283-246)	Antiochus I (281/280-261)	Manasseh

First Syrian War (274-272)

Antiochus II   Onias II
(261-246)

Second Syrian War   (Joseph the Tobiad)
(260-252)

Ptolemy III Euergetes   Seleucus II
(246-221)   (246-226)

Third Syrian War (246-241)

Seleucus III
(226-223)

Ptolemy IV Philopator   Antiochus III   Simeon II
(221-204)   (223-187)   (220-190)

Fourth Syrian War (221-217)

Ptolemy V Epiphanes
(204-180)

Fifth Syrian War (201-198)

The Seleucid Era (198-167 BC)

Antiochus conquers Greek cities
(193)

Driven from Greece (192) Onias III
(190-174)

Defeated by Rome (188)
(Peace of Apemea)

(Conflict with
Simon, Temple-
Captain)

Ptolemy VI (181-145)   Seleucus IV
         Philopator
         (187-175)

                 Antiochus IV   Jason (175-172)
                 Epiphanes
                 (175-164)
           Antiochus' Egyptian campaigns (169-168)

                                     Menelaus (172-162)

The Maccabean Revolt (167-142 BC)

Egypt	*Syria*	*Judea*	*(High-Priest)*
		Judas Maccabeus (167-161)	
		Dedication of the Temple (165)	
	Antiochus V Eupator (164-162)	Syria Peace Treaty (163/162)	
		Roman Treaty (162/161)	
	Demetrius I (162-150)	Jonathan (161-142)	Alcimus (162-159)
			Intersacerdotum (159-152)
	Alexander Balas (150-145)		Jonathan (152-142)
Ptolemy VIII (145)	Demetrius II (145-138)		
Ptolemy VIII (145-116)	Antiochus VI (145-142)		
	Trypho (142-138)		

The Hasmonean Period (142-63 BC)

Egypt	*Syria*	*Jerusalem and Judea*
		Simon (142-135/34)
	Demetrius captive in Parthia (139-128)	
	Antiochus VII (138-128)	John Hyrcanus (135/34-104)
	Campaigns in Judea, Samaria, and Idumea	
	Demetrius II (128-125)	
	Antiochus VIII (125-113)	
	Antiochus IX (113-95)	
	Conquest of Iturea	
		Conquest of Samaria and Idumea
Ptolemy IX (116-107)		
Cleopatra III (107-101)		Aristobulus I (104-103)
		Alexander Jannaeus (103-76)
Ptolemy X (101-88)	Demetrius III (95-87)	Coastal Plain captured (ca. 95)
		Civil war (ca. 88)

Antiochus XII
(86-84)

Salome Alexandra (76-67)
    Hyrcanus II, High-priest
    (76-67)

Syria made   Aristobulus II (67-63)
    a Roman
    province (64)

Pompey conquers Jerusalem (63)

The Early Roman Period (63-4 BC)

Rome	Syria	Palestine
	Scaurus, Governor (65-62)	Hyrcanus II, High-priest (63-40)
Triumvirate: Pompey, Crassus, Caesar (60-53)	Gabinius, Governor (57-55)	
	Crassus, Governor (55-53)	Antipater, Procurator (55-43)
Crassus killed (53) Pompey defeated (48)	Cassius (53-51,44-42)	Hyrcanus II, Ethnarch (47-40)
Caesar, Dictator (45-44)		
Triumvirate: Antony, Lepidus Octavian (43-36)		Phasael, Governor of Judea (ca. 43-40) Herod, Governor of Galilee (ca. 43-40)

Antigonus, King and High-priest
(40-37)

Herod, King (37-4)

Hananel, High-
priest (37)

Aristobulus, High-
priest (37)

Hananel, High-
priest (36-30)

Octavian (Augustus)   Boethus, High-
  sole ruler   priest (24-4)
  (27 BC-AD 14)

Temple construction begun
(ca. 20/19)

The New Testament Era (4 BC-AD 66)

Rome	Judea and Samaria	Galilee and Perea	Northern Transjordan
	Archelaus Ethnarch (4 BC-AD 6)	Herod Antipas Tetrarch (4 BC-AD 39)	Philip, Tetrarch (4 BC-AD 34)
	Procurators:		
	Coponius (6-9)		
	Ambibulus (9-12)		
Tiberius (14-37)	Rufus (12-15)		
	Valerius Gratus (15-36)		

Sejanus executed (31)	Pontius Pilate (26-36)	
	Marcellus (36)	Syrian Rule (34-37)
Caligula (37-41)	Marullus (37-41)	Agrippa I, King (37-44)
Claudius (41-54)	Agrippa I, King (41-44) Agrippa I King (40-44)	
	Procurators:	
	Cuspius Fadus (44-46)	
	Theudas emerges (45)	
	Tiberius Alexander (46-48)	
	Famine (ca. 46)	
	Ventidus Cumanus (48-52)	Agrippa II (49-92/93) King of Chalcis (49)
	Felix (52-60)	Philip's tetrarchy added (53)
		Galilee and Perea added (54/55)
Nero (54-68) Rome burns (64)	Paul arrested (ca. 58)	
	Festus (60-62)	

Albinus (62-64)

Florus (64-66)

The Final Days of the Hebrew Nation (AD 66-135)

Rome	Palestine
	First Jewish Revolt (66-74)
Galba (68-69)	Vespasian conquers Galilee (67), Perea and part of Judea (68)
Otho (69)	
Vitellius (69)	
Vespasian (69-79)	Jerusalem falls (70)
	Brassus, Governor (71-73)
	Silva, Governor (73-81)
	Fall of Masada (74)
	The period of Jabneh (74-132)
	Johanan ben Zakkai (74-80)
Titus (79-81)	Gamaliel (80-120)
Domitian (81-96)	
Persecution of Christians (96)	
Nerva (96-98)	
Trajan (98-117)	Quietus, Governor (117)
Hadrian (117-138)	Bar Kochba Revolt (132-135)
	Fall of Bethar (135)

Bibliography

Bevan, Edwyn. *Jerusalem under the High Priests.* London: Edward Arnold Ltd., 1958.

Bruce, F. F. *Israel and the Nations.* Exeter: The Paternoster Press, 1975.

Collins, John J. *Between Athens and Jerusalem.* New York: Crossroads, 1986.

Davies, Philip R. *Qumran.* Guilford: Lutterworth Press, 1982.

Ellison, H. L. *From Babylon to Bethlehem.* Exeter: The Paternoster Press, 1976.

Foakes-Jackson, F. J. *Josephus and the Jews.* London: SPCK, 1930.

Forster, Werner. *Palestinian Judaism in New Testament Times,* G. E. Harris, trans. London: Oliver and Boyd, 1964.

Hengel, Martin. *Jews, Greeks, and Barbarians.* London: SCM Press, 1980.

Jagersma, H. *A History of Israel from Alexander the Great to Bar Kochba.* London: SCM Press,1985.

Jones, A. H. M. *The Herods of Judea.* Oxford: Clarendon Press, 1938.

Leaney, A. R. C. *The Jewish and Christian World: 200 B.C. to A.D. 200.* Cambridge: Cambridge University Press, 1984.

McCullough, W. Stewart. *The History and Literature of the Palestinian Jews from Cyrus to Herod.* Toronto: University of Toronto Press, 1975.

Oesterly, W. O. E. *A History of Israel,* vol. II. Oxford: Clarendon Press, 1932.

Reicke, Bo. *The New Testament Era: The World of the Bible from 500 B.C. to A.D. 100,* David E. Green, trans. Philadelphia: Fortress Press, 1964.

Russell, D. S. *Between the Testaments.* London: SCM Press, 1960.

_____. *From Early Judaism to Early Church.* London: SCM Press, 1986.

Schurer, Emil. *The History of the Jewish People in the Age of Jesus Christ (175 B.C.-A.D. 135),* revised by Geza Vermes and Fergus Millar (3 vols.). Edinburgh: T. & T. Clark Ltd., 1973-1986.

Stauffer, Ethelbert. *Jesus and His Story,* Richard and Clara Winston, trans. New York: Alfred A. Knopf, 1960.

Stone, Michael, Edward. *Scriptures, Sects, and Visions.* Philadelphia: Fortress Press, 1980.

Vermes, Geza. *The Dead Sea Scrolls: Qumran in Perspective.* London: Collins, 1977.

Indexes

Names and Places